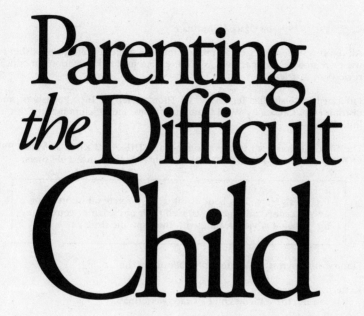

Parenting the Difficult Child

Grace Ketterman, M.D.

OLIVER
NELSON

THOMAS NELSON PUBLISHERS
Nashville • Atlanta • London • Vancouver

Published in Nashville, Tennessee, by Thomas Nelson, Inc., Publishers, and distributed in Canada by Word Communications, Ltd., Richmond, British Columbia.

The Bible version used in this publication is THE NEW KING JAMES VERSION. Copyright © 1979, 1980, 1982, Thomas Nelson, Inc., Publishers.

PUBLISHER'S NOTE: This book is intended for general information only. Readers are urged to consult their physician or counselor for personal advice dealing with their specific situation.

Library of Congress Cataloging-in-Publication Data

Ketterman, Grace H.
    Parenting the difficult child / Grace Ketterman.
        p.   cm.
    Includes bibliographical references
    ISBN 0-8407-9130-5
    1. Problem children.   2. Child rearing.   3. Child psychology.
I. Title.
HQ773.K47   1994
649'.153—dc20   94-17849
                                                           CIP

Printed in the United States of America.

2   3   4   5   6   —   99   98   97   96   95

Contents

Symptoms of Trouble: *Moodiness, Withdrawal, Conduct
Disorders, Grief and Depression, Emotional Disorders,
Oppositional or Defiant Disorders;* Dealing with the
Difficult Teen: *Foster Independence, Expand the
Boundaries, Show Respect, Listen, Share Yourself;* Let's
Get Specific: *Moodiness, Withdrawal, Conduct Disorders,
Grief and Depression, Emotional Disorders, Oppositional or
Defiant Disorders;* Get Some Help

Introduction:
That Difficult
Child

More than four decades ago, I began to work professionally with children with special needs and problems. Whether those concerns were physical, emotional, or interpersonal was irrelevant. They and their families were in pain. As a pediatrician and psychiatrist, I had the responsibility and opportunity to analyze, diagnose, and treat the conditions causing their pain.

Many times such diagnoses were simple—a lab test diagnosed a strep throat. A personal and family history revealed a child's grief or depression. The treatment, then, was easy and the results, successful. A grateful family and healed patient presented a special reward, prompting me to continue to strive for success with increasingly difficult challenges.

Over the years, however, I have discovered some hard-core concerns that are not so readily solvable. These concerns emanate from children and adolescents whose impact on their parents and other adults is habitually painful. They are the ones who seem to move persistently under a troublesome dark cloud that rains on the parades of others.

Nine-year-old Joe was one of those kids. He played really hard. His jeans wore through at the knees, and his shirt buttons vanished so often that his mother was kept busy replacing them. Joe was the object of more lectures, after-school detentions, and lengthy groundings than any of his three siblings. He was sick more often, more seriously ill, and much more difficult to care for than they. When Joe lost a game, he refused to play his opponent again. When his grades were less than the quality he wanted, he blamed his "lousy" teachers and declared that they "had it in" for him. He teased his younger sister and resisted the entreaties of his mother.

Joe's dad, with his booming voice and no-nonsense manner, could usually get him to comply. But his long-suffering mother was often unable to do so. Joe felt so angry and hurt by her alternate reminding or giving up that he confided, "I hate her! And I think she hates me!"

Joe is an example of a difficult child. Wherever he goes, there is tension—if not outright gloom. All too often this dark cloud is accented by an angelic little sister who can do no wrong. And Joe learns to taunt and harass her out of his own unfavorable self-comparison.

Joe and his family, and usually his teacher and schoolmates, live in misery. If you are a parent of such a child, boy or girl, you know that misery all too well. You almost certainly have suffered the guilt of blaming yourself and the frustration of blaming your spouse. Both of you have often blamed your child.

The difficult child is easily identified by parents who live with one! Here are some of the characteristics of this type of child. Every difficult child does not evidence all of these, but when four or more of these traits are present, you will know you have a difficult child on your hands.

1. *Unpredictability*. At one time the child will be cooperative and pleasant. On other occasions only anger and defiance will be demonstrated.
2. *Opposition*. When parents declare the blue sky and sunshine predict a lovely day, this child will insist that the sky is gray and that it's going to rain. The stubbornness and defiance that go with this quality can be almost unbearable.
3. *Quick and explosive anger*. Difficult children do not always display this trait, but it is common. They often are highly destructive during the tantrum.
4. *Moodiness and/or grouchiness*. Parents of difficult children often describe that they feel as if they are "walking on eggshells." There may be no apparent reason for the moods.
5. *Offensiveness*. Behaviors range from giddy or silly to rude, but these difficult children offend most of the people around them. They are lonely and friendless.
6. *Restlessness and/or boredom*. Difficult children are often on the go, seek excitement, and avoid boredom at any cost.
7. *Withdrawal and silence*. Depending on the personality bent, difficult kids may refuse to talk or respond to overtures of any kind. This surly demeanor is

often more troublesome to cope with than more overt misbehaviors.

No matter what combination of these traits your child manifests, this book will help you. It will enable you to understand that difficult kids are not really impossible to deal with. You will discover that you were not the champion Parent Failure of the Year.

Difficult kids are just different from their parents' expectations. And they require special handling and clear understanding. With individualized methods, they blossom into wonderful people. Try it and see!

You recall that Joe expressed feeling hatred between himself and his mother. Many difficult children and their parents share similar emotions. Through understanding and accurate information, such painful, negative feelings may be replaced with deep love and even enjoyment.

1

Just Like Uncle Raymond!

There are some difficulties with which a child is born. They are "ready made" on arrival. Others develop in response to parents' misunderstandings, misperceptions, or mistakes. The latter are much more readily solved than the former. Edward is an example that may help you determine which problem is confronting you.

Even at birth, he resembled Uncle Raymond. Both grandmother and grandfather agreed that the set of his ears, the broad forehead, and the prominent chin depicted the family traits of this uncle.

Baby Edward (a name carefully chosen to avoid the sounds of "Raymond!") was unfortunately labeled at birth. He did show similarities to the family's "irregular" person. Uncle Raymond had been a pushy child of whom most cousins were afraid. He developed into an obnoxious schoolboy who antagonized his classmates.

By adolescence, Raymond was clearly becoming an

arrogant know-it-all whom no one could stand. Despite his intelligence and determined spirit, others saw him as intolerably ego-centered.

It was with great dread that Edward's parents listened to the grandparents' pronouncement of resemblance! They knew only the embellished stories of Uncle Raymond since they had never lived close to him. But they understood enough to vow their son would never grow up to be like him.

As Edward grew, he naturally showed progress toward early childhood's first signs of independence. *Oh, no!* thought his father. *We won't allow him to become like Raymond.* So they held Edward close to them, creating tight boundaries around him. When he reached for toys other children were playing with in the nursery, they pulled him firmly away. Edward would never become the grabby, antagonistic person Raymond allegedly had been.

When Edward, at age two, began to overuse the response of "No!" his parents heard the echoes of Raymond's touted arrogance. They forgot that all two-year-olds try out this word just to see the response it elicits. Again and again, they stifled Edward's normal and necessary stretch for healthy individuality.

As time went on, Edward did begin to resemble his relative. Subjected to his parents' intense controls, he learned to fight against them using their methods. The more belligerent they seemed, the more angry he acted. In adolescence, Edward began to stay out late. He chose friends who missed school all too often, and he broke a number of rules at school.

Edward's parents believed he had inherited Uncle

Raymond's genes and chromosomes, and they never admitted that part of his problems came from their negative expectations. Their attitude, communication, and
demeanor reflected their worry. Adults know that worry
and concern come from love for a child. To a child, however, they clearly state, "You have a big, bad problem."
A child usually translates that to mean, "*I* am bad!"
Having the name all too commonly translates into playing the game.

Let me insert some comments here to reassure you
that I'm not from the permissive, anything-goes school!
Even the most compliant two-year-olds must be corrected and restrained to prevent them from trying to run
their world into disaster. But giving too little freedom
and too much control can be even more disastrous.
When parents' control emanates from the fear that their
child could become a person with deplorably bad conduct, the results are predictable. They will be more than
likely to create the unpleasant characteristics they fear.

■

WHAT'S A PARENT TO DO?

I f you have a child who resembles a relative of unsa-
vory personality, here are some ideas to help you.

■ Discover Positive Resemblances

Look carefully at your child's features. Define each one,
and then look at photographs of your relatives—those
you love a lot and those you love a lot less. If you keep
an open mind, the chances are, you'll find some charac-

teristics of several family members. Consciously keep in your thoughts the positive resemblances instead of the negative ones.

■ Research the Family Tree

If you see your child unmistakably growing to look like that problem relative, research the family tree. Acquire all the facts you can about the relative. How did she grow up? How did his family treat him? Was she successful, or did she hide her fear of failure behind a mask of rudeness? Although many traits are inherited, I have yet to hear of a chromosome for obnoxiousness! You may, in fact, unearth some forgotten goodness in this "bad" person. At any rate, physical resemblances are not tied to personality traits.

■ Respect Emerging Traits

Explore with an unbiased mind who your child is becoming. Always look for the positive aspect of an emerging trait. The strong-willed child is a fine example. This quality, so often seen as a negative one, may be instead the root of greatness. Such a child clashes intensely from early months with his strong-willed parent. If you are one of those parents, you may see your child becoming more and more like your own dominating, controlling parent. Failing to see this characteristic in yourself, you may struggle to break the child's will so he won't become like that other person.

True enough, sometimes we all must bend our wills to God's and someone else's. But in the process of breaking your child's will, you may damage her spirit. The end result may be an embittered, rebellious child who behaves exactly as you wanted her not to do!

Rather than worrying over your child's strong will or any negative trait, try being grateful for it. Find ways to train that will to develop into the tenacity that will accomplish noteworthy things. One way you can do this is to point out your respect for his opinion. You can even explain that you wish you could always give in to him because that would be easier, but at times your experience allows you to know his opinion is not right. And because you love him so much, you simply won't give in.

■ Seek Counseling

If you have already begun this damaging process, hold everything! Seek an experienced family counselor who can help you regain perspective. Seeing yourself as well as your child and those she resembles can help you see clearly how to correct the mistakes you have made.

■ Practice Unconditional Love

Practice unconditional love, no matter whom your child resembles or how he acts. In the famous summary of love from the Bible, we are told, "Love believes all things" (1 Cor. 13:7). Only recently have I understood this statement. Many parents believe only the positives about the child because they can accept and love her only if she is perfect. Conversely, if they must admit there are negative qualities in a child, they reject her. The rejection may be unconscious, but a child will quickly sense such feelings and will respond by rebelling or withdrawing.

Healthy, unconditional love reacts quite differently. It says, "I see that you are sometimes kind and trustworthy. And I see at other times that you behave rudely and act dishonestly. In fact, you can be downright sneaky! I love you, no matter how you behave, but when your actions are hurtful, you can count on my correcting you." That is the essence of tough, unconditional love. Learn to practice it, and your child will learn to respect and honor you.

∎ Rely on God's Love

Whether the difficulties you experience with your child are inborn or caused by unconscious misperceptions and mistakes, they will complicate your task of parenting. It is never easy to be a competent, successful parent. When you face any special challenge, your job becomes even more strenuous. But you have access to the Power far beyond your own. Discover and draw upon the love and wisdom of God, and you will make it!

2

The Child
of Divorce

For many classroom teachers, over 60 percent of their students come from families that have been through a divorce. However it is studied and reduced to cold numbers, there is no possible way to measure the impact of divorce on the lives of children and parents.

All too commonly the issues that initiated the relentlessly widening chasm ending in divorce are never resolved and the wounds are not healed. Parents continue their battles through their children, catching them in the crossfire.

Richard was typical of many children who suffer from the trauma of divorce. When I knew him, he was fourteen—a handsome young man with an angry demeanor and a bag full of mean tricks. He could look at a teacher with such scorn that it ruined her day. He could imply threats that would prompt one to seek a police escort at all times. Both physically and emotionally, other children shrank from his presence. Richard was a difficult child who contaminated every group of which he was a part.

Repeatedly, I tried to chip away at the layers of protective barnacles that the seas of the boy's life had formed. The rough points often injured me as they had others. But I was too tough and far too stubborn to give up.

One day, after an hour of tolerating Richard's rude attacks, I heard him say, "Maybe I don't deserve to live at all!" The profoundly frightening idea seemed to emerge like a thunderbolt from a cloudless sky. But it was the breakthrough for which I had waited.

"Perhaps," I said, "it isn't you who shouldn't live. Maybe you think it's your dad who deserves not to live. He did some really mean things, didn't he?"

Anger, anguish, and tears mixed together in Richard's eyes and voice as he finally admitted some basic truths. His father, an alcoholic, abandoned the family of five when Richard was only a baby. Over the years of his childhood, Richard learned that his father had abused his mother and older brothers and sister. He knew the memories were too painful for his mom to discuss, but he recognized her protective anger and learned to copy it. Rather than feel weak or vulnerable, he learned to attack first and not wait to be hurt by others. His anger pervaded his entire life, becoming the severe emotional reaction that made others avoid him.

Another troubling issue to Richard was easy to discover once he talked about his life. Richard strongly resembled his massive, abusive father. Again and again he'd heard the words: "Son, you're the spitting image of your father. If you're not careful, you'll grow to be just like him!" In those words, Richard heard not a threat but a curse: "Just like Dad! Mean! Abusive! Irresponsible! A fighter."

Richard wanted to become a strong, powerful man. So he practiced acting like the powerful man about whom he had heard so much. If he looked like Dad, he probably had inherited Dad's personality. No doubt he was doomed to be like the father he had known only from others' harsh descriptions—at least that's what Richard thought.

■
TAKE PREVENTIVE MEASURES

How common such thinking is! I have interviewed many young people in attempts to explore their problems and find the answers. Almost always I learn that in similar situations, kids think like Richard. If they repeatedly hear that they look like their missing parent (the "mean" one), they learn to believe they are powerless to become anything else. And so it is that a difficult parent creates a difficult child.

There is a major preventive force against such an event's happening. That power lies in the reach of the parent who has custody and actually raises the child. Other relatives and family friends can be helpful, too. Here are the steps that will work.

■ Forgive

Be mature enough to forgive the erring spouse. Even when there is the heartache of separation and divorce, find the grace to offer forgiveness. Even when your ex is totally at fault (a rarity indeed!), forgive! Through genuine forgiveness alone, you can be sure to avoid the judgmental comments and attitudes that can spill over on your child.

■ Gather Information

Take the trouble to gather information about the offending partner. Can you identify any elements that played a part in producing the adult you know? How could your ex have been different if the formative years had been more successful or if the discipline had been more fair or consistent? Such information will enable you to forgive more profoundly and will revolutionize your attitude. Think how a positive, understanding attitude toward the other parent will affect your child.

■ Look for the Good

Look for all the good qualities in your ex-spouse. Estranged spouses struggle with this step because they have focused so intently on the problems for a long time. You may have to go back to your courtship and honeymoon. Just do it! Then start telling your child about the good qualities. When you see them in your child, remember to compliment her.

■ Face Personal Faults and Mistakes

Face your faults and mistakes. Whenever your child points them out or whenever you stumble so badly you can't deny your imperfections, admit them graciously. You can then take two further steps:

1. Correct those mistakes, and work to overcome your weaknesses whenever that's possible.
2. In confessing your errors to your critical child, reassure her that she need not copy your faults. Encourage her to avoid such flaws and to remind you to overcome them whenever you slip.

These steps will help your child learn from the faults of both parents instead of repeating them. And you are free from any possibility of putting down anyone. That's not a bad philosophy to live by!

■ Point Out Strengths

In every aspect of your child's life, look for his strengths more than the weak spots. Certainly, the latter must be corrected and strengthened. But the best tool for making such improvements is your belief in the assets that are present in every child. As you recognize them and teach your child to value them, both of you can draw on them to live successfully.

■

REACTIONS TO DIVORCE

It's not just the resemblance to the missing "mean" parent that helps create the difficult child of divorce. Negative emotions are the expected by-products of the fermenting anger of the divorcing couple. The arguments, accusations, and counterattacks of the total environment before, during, and after the divorce are distressing to everyone, but children are especially vulnerable.

■ Aggressiveness

Some children of divorce cry, yell, and live out the pain of the losses divorce creates. They usually act angry and become aggressive, even destructive. Perhaps such behaviors alleviate their sense of helplessness and allow them temporarily to feel some power. An adult, trying to cope with a child in this frame of mind, often misinterprets the behaviors. The adult punishes and tries to avoid the difficult child, creating more fear and resulting in further acting out.

■ Withdrawal

Other children of divorce hide their pain in silent withdrawing. They may deny the loss and pretend they like it better with Dad (or Mom) gone. At least they no longer have to hear the arguments. But the energy demanded by such denial leaves many of these kids exhausted. Their schoolwork suffers, their social life deteriorates, and their grief grows to become depression. Depressed kids are full of the mixed feelings of guilt, anxiety, worry, anger, sadness and, ultimately, helplessness. They fear their parents' problems were somehow their fault. Such false guilt often leads to low self-esteem and fear of failure. These kids tend to give up in silent despair.

■ Premature Parenting

And still other children of divorce become premature parents. Their efforts and energy are siphoned off as they try to parent their parents, siblings, and grandparents. Loving and conscientious to a fault, these children suffer serious personal losses. Heroically, they attempt to rebuild some security by taking care of everyone else. The effort seems altruistic and even commendable.

But think with me for a moment. Almost all of us like the sweetness of sugar. But when its concentration in the bloodstream becomes too high, a person may die. In the same way, excessive caretaking of others, sweet as it seems, can become harmful. The *too* good, *too* caring child may be at grave risk, and she may be negatively affecting others through fostering dependency and stunting healthy emotional growth in them.

■ Escape Is *Not* the Way

The ultimate destructive effect of divorce stems from the poor role modeling. When a child sees his parent escaping the usual conflicts of life through divorce instead of working them out, he may come to believe escape is normal. A child best learns the skills for building a strong marriage by observing one and for establishing a healthy family by living in one! Without a parent who models the way to stick to a relationship and work out problems, how can a child learn?

Certainly, there are a few truly unhealthy marriages that need to be dissolved. Many of us have great difficulty seeing that divorce is *ever* an acceptable decision. Over time, however, I have worked with a few families where the abuse and neglect were so marked that the safety of children demanded the removal of the dangerous parent.

Only when counseling and legal interventions fail to effect adequate change is divorce (or at least separation) justifiable.

Obtaining help for a troubled marriage requires a concerted effort in today's culture. There has come to be a highly permissive attitude among counselors that makes divorce easier and more appealing than the work of mending weak areas in the relationship. Here are some suggestions:

1. Both spouses need to go to an experienced, well-trained marriage and family therapist. Seek one who believes in marriage, who can be impartial, and who understands the working of the family as a system.
2. If one spouse refuses to cooperate, the other needs to go alone to the same type of counselor. If one spouse changes for the better, the other is likely to improve.
3. Patience and endurance through difficult times can help a couple outlast stormy periods. One who

reaches an even keel often helps the other return to a healthy relationship.

4. Know when marriage turns into a dangerous situation, risking emotional, physical, or even spiritual health for children. Tough love may have to prompt separation.

5. Always pray for divine guidance, healing, and strength.

If separation is inevitable and reconciliation is impossible, understanding and forgiving are healing forces.

Children rarely understand divorce and nearly always are hurt by it (the exception being breaking a cycle of serious abuse). When staying together is no longer an option, these steps can help prevent most of the damage to the children:

1. Explain honestly and tactfully why the separation was necessary. Make this clear enough to keep the children from blaming themselves but not so detailed they lose all respect for the parent.

2. Help the children through their grief over the loss of the family, especially the missing parent.

3. Teach the children to avoid the mistakes their parents made and yet to honor and emulate the good qualities.

4. Work out a fair amount of time with both parents so the children don't have to lose totally the parent who leaves.

5. Avoid condemning or even criticizing the other parent to, or in the hearing of, the children. Instead, point out the positive attributes of that par-

ent because children may feel they are like that person.

Teaching your child to love, forgive, and respect her parents even when they are imperfect is quite a challenge. But this concept will enable her to respect herself and you in a healthy way.

Do everything possible to save your marriage and make it strong. When this is not possible, seek a separation that is clearly necessary, achieve the healing God can give, and move on.

3

She's Just
Like Me

Anita wanted to be on the girls' volleyball team. She practiced in her backyard with friends until she exhausted them, so they began to avoid her. She talked about playing in the school tournaments until even her mother grew weary of hearing it. Anita was an intense person, wanting whatever impressed her at the moment with every fiber of her being.

In spite of her work and wishes, Anita did not make the team. She was devastated. She wailed out her grief and all of the anger attending it. Each reaction was in keeping with her temperament. The family shared her disappointment, but Faye, her mother, was most upset. She railed at the coach and officially complained to the school administrators.

It was sad that Anita couldn't get on the volleyball team. But in a few days, she was happily going swimming and eating burgers with her friends.

Faye was the one who struggled to recover from the letdown. She continued to feel sad and angry. When even Anita began to question her, Faye took time to think. After only a moment, her own adolescent experiences flooded her consciousness. She had wanted to be on her school's swim team, but she failed to measure up and was cut. The tragedy of her failure had resulted in prolonged criticism from her father. He saw no fault with the coach, but he blamed Faye for not trying hard enough. To her, Dad's attitude multiplied her failure. She had let him, her teammates, the coach, and her whole school down. She felt disgraced for years—until time slowly erased those dreadful memories.

Anita's failure jolted those early events into vivid recall of their tragic impact on Faye's life. She vowed her daughter should not have to experience her pain. So she urged her on, encouraged her, and went to bat for her. Mom's girlhood struggles made her feed into Anita some of the intensity of her daughter's wishes, efforts, and reactions.

The truth was, however, that the mother read far more in Anita's disappointment than the daughter really felt. When Faye saw the look of disappointment in her child's face, watched her tears, and shared in her grief, much of her hurt was for her own past. She automatically presumed that Anita felt just like she had so many years before. Anita was upset, but in a short while she moved on with life, compensating with other successes for the failure.

In this case, the problem lay within the heart of the mother. The abusive response of her father had marred Faye's youth, leaving scars on her adult life. Unconsciously, she believed her child would duplicate her own pain. Fortunately, that was not true. But some of the credit for Anita's healthier responses lay in Mom's efforts to make things right despite her own remembered pain.

INNER RESEMBLANCES CAN CAUSE CRISES

It is almost universally true that parents read some of themselves into their kids. There are clear genetic resemblances that set the stage for this unconscious drama. Mannerisms, habits, and other traits enhance the belief that a child not only looks and acts like the parent but is, in fact, like her.

In the case of Anita and Faye, the resemblance caused considerable pressure on the daughter, but the real pain was mostly Mom's. In other situations, however, a child's resemblance to the parent can become an overwhelming obstacle in that youngster's life.

Beverly was caught up in such a situation. Her mother, Vicki, was prone to venting her vicious temper. The entire family lived in dread of Vicki's explosions. One by one, her in-laws stopped attending family functions, and Vicki, in turn, became even more attacking and angry.

As Beverly grew up, she learned not to give in to Mom's anger but to confront it. The two clashed in savage fury over even minor issues. During adolescence, Beverly attended a boarding school to try to cool their fiery relationship.

Although that separation alleviated their struggles and

enabled Beverly to get through her teens, it did not eradicate the negatives in her heart. As an adult, she and Vicki are still bitter opponents, still waging the wars of her youth.

It was clear that Vicki taught her child how to be angry. When she recognized the ugliness of Beverly's behavior, she tried to correct her child. But she failed to see her role as teacher and to change her own behavior and attitudes. Even in attempting to correct Beverly, Vicki used her violent anger, and she abused her daughter through screaming fits. She called Beverly names and pointed out her faults. Her behavior didn't guide her child to more positive behaviors.

Beverly was stuck, along with her mother, in the anger that flowed across many generations. Negative emotions in children are often, but not always, instilled in them by parents.

If you see traits in your child that you do not like, you may be like Vicki. Take a look at yourself. If you don't like what you see, take action!

■

CHANGE IS POSSIBLE

A dear friend debates with me people's ability to change. He insists that no one really changes after early childhood. I am certain that people can and do change dramatically. And perhaps both of us are correct.

Basic temperaments are inborn, say the long-term studies of some child specialists. The personality of every person is clearly definable by the age of three, say other students of children. Their research confirms that they are right.

Nevertheless, the entire field of mental health is based on the evidence that people's behaviors, insights, and attitudes can change. Furthermore, when people learn to think straight and take charge of their actions, new, healthy feelings and attitudes will follow.

If your child demonstrates attitudes and behaviors that seriously annoy you, take a long look at yourself. Can you find traces of the same traits in yourself? Perhaps there are vast quantities of them.

You may have worked at changing some of your difficult behaviors in the past, and you really do not see them currently. Your child may have learned the annoying behaviors from others. Yet the reminder of your old habits can be most frustrating. In either event, here are some steps for you to take.

■ Review

Review your behaviors and the way you express your emotions. If you see that they resemble your child's negative behaviors and speech, you have made a vital discovery. Your child must change behaviors—and so must you! It is a waste of energy to try to convince your child to stop yelling while you are screaming. Stop screaming!

No matter how good a parent you are or even how committed you are as a Christian, it is entirely possible you may have been angrier with your child than you intended to be. It is the intensity of your emotional reaction as well as your tone of voice that could be damaging your parenting skills.

■ Confess

Confess your mistakes to your child. He is well aware of them anyway, so you need not worry about his losing respect for you. He will discover a new respect once he recovers from his surprise.

■ Plan

Formulate your plan for changing. In case you have been screaming, what will you do instead? I suggest taking time out for yourself. Get away and think about the issue that upsets you, what your child needs to learn about it, and how that learning can take place most effectively. It is likely you and God together will discover more effective methods for correcting your child!

■ Act

When you are back in control and have established your plan, return to your child. In the Old Testament, these powerful words appear: "In quietness and confidence shall be your strength" (Isa. 30:15). Talk calmly, even firmly if you must, about the situation until it is resolved. Let me remind you that many children respond better to action than they do to talk. Lead your child to the assigned task, or at the end of a program, turn off the TV if your child needs to study.

It is okay for you to be in charge! Respect your child, and teach him to respect you. You may do that best by believing in the strength of your experience and wisdom and knowing that God intended parents to be the human authority.

Teachers of all grades affirm my experiences. The lack of respect from young people for themselves, each other, and adults is a major problem. Much of this problem could be alleviated by teaching respect at home. Such teaching must involve healthy authority in parents. When parents are reasonable, strong, and consistent in both modeling and requiring respect, a child will usually learn that quality.

■
REPLACE THE NEGATIVES WITH THE POSITIVES

In guiding and disciplining your child, use clear thinking, firm action, and patient persistence. When your child knows you will show her how to act thoughtfully and considerately, the old negative reactions will subside. Breaking habits is a long and laborious process. Be patient with yourself and your child. Each of you will fall back into old habits at times. But with tolerance and forgiveness, you will make new, healthy habits emerge.

Whatever the fault you deplore, you can overcome it with courage, planning, and determination. You may require professional counseling, but the changes will be well worth all your efforts.

4

The Lazy Child

Janice wrote this note: "My fourteen-year-old child seems to be unmotivated. She failed sixth grade and now in the eighth grade is failing at least one class. She only wants to watch TV or listen to rotten music. She's critical and unhappy, so disruptive to our family. It's affecting all of us!"

This adolescent is typical of a large number of unmotivated children. Their so-called laziness makes teachers want to change professions and makes parents wish they could!

The laziness of a child like Brenda enrages her siblings as well as her parents and teachers. Eleven-year-old Brenda loved to read and watch TV. She had few friends and preferred to be alone. She greatly disliked doing household tasks and usually found a way to dump her few assigned responsibilities on her older sister. Brenda had a powerful ally. She was her father's favorite child, and early on, she discovered he would take her side. He excused her as being too young to do such big tasks.

Her refusal to work and her constant ability to be sheltered by her indulgent father created untold anger in the rest of the family. Even her mother became angry and found herself powerless to effect a change in Brenda's slothfulness.

Laziness, sloth, or lack of motivation is a deplorable condition that is widespread. It may be evident on the job where teens, in part-time employment, try to get by with the least work possible. They take extended breaks, talk with each other, watch the clock, and passively let others carry the biggest load. These, by the way, are practices many adults follow, too!

At home, laziness may be either passive or deliberate. Children conveniently "forget" to do assigned tasks and slip away to play with friends or read books. They realize, in many cases, that their failure to help puts unfair burdens on their parents. Many even feel guilty, but their laziness is so powerful, they seem incapable of change, even to overcome their guilt.

In school, laziness creates problems with lifelong repercussions. Youngsters who refuse to study and fail, like Janice's daughter, may dangerously limit their future options. With the low grades they earn, lazy kids risk rejection from colleges, and the good jobs will usually go to others. These kids even lose respect from peers who are motivated. These lazy young people may band together in groups that become involved in antisocial activities. Often these young people have told me they like only fun and excitement. They will replace success and the effort that achieving success requires with the easy habits of pleasure.

■

WHY?

■ Rebellion

Another letter reveals some insights into a teenager's dilemma. Here is a piece of the puzzle her mother found: "Kelli [the daughter] and her father fight continually, and I feel I'm losing the closeness I once felt with her. Her father does not agree with me on getting some kind of help."

In many cases, so-called laziness is a symptom of rebellion. (See chapter 15 on rebellion.) It is a passive means of getting even with an overpowering parent. Kelli and her father are in opposition most of the time. Her father is a formidable foe whom she cannot beat in fair fights. He always wins, but he fails to realize that he is fast losing the war. By doing nothing and by exhibiting rebellious behaviors, she is showing her world daily, "Dad thinks he's the boss, but he can't make me do anything I don't want to do!"

Parents do not intend to launch battles with their children. They only want to see them do the right and responsible things. But inadvertently, they slip into the power struggles that become a war. Once battle lines are drawn, parents believe they dare not lose. The truth is, all too commonly, both parent and child do lose.

The best way to cope with this kind of negative behavior is to exhibit love. If only Kelli's dad would show his child affection and small areas of pride in her, a miracle would take place. But even Mother's love is no match for Dad's anger. In trying to support his discipline, Mom has joined the "enemy," and her loved child is becoming estranged from her. Small wonder these parents are considering placing their "lazy" daughter in a convenient treatment center for teens. (When parent-child conflicts reach a serious impasse, short-term separation of the child from the parent can be useful.) All too often, the problem of laziness has its origin in the power struggles between parent and child.

■ Parental Protection

Brenda's laziness, on the other hand, had two components. First is the natural tendency of most children, especially younger ones, to prefer the easy life. Few kids automatically pitch in and help with hard work. There is a universal wish to be taken care of, to laugh and play and have others provide. She certainly evidenced that propensity.

For Brenda, however, there was a more far-reaching reason. It lay in her father's vulnerability to her charms. She knew exactly how to say and do the things that pleased him. When anyone else criticized Dad, Brenda defended him. She teased away some of his worries, and in exchange, he protected her from learning to be responsible. She was Daddy's little girl. Even Mom's kindly firmness was no match for their tight alliance.

■ **Perfectionism**

Yet another reason for laziness is one that is truly a paradox. Many children become lazy because they are perfectionists. Due to their temperaments and their training, these young people want everything to be exactly right!

They will attempt to do a school project, but while researching the project, they hit a difficult spot. Unable to find exactly the needed information, they become discouraged, feel defeated, and may freeze in their sense of helplessness. If it's not perfect, it's no good at all.

Nan lived with an amazingly perfectionist father. With good intentions, but distressing methods, he demanded total perfection—and perfect was his only way. Although he tried to be patient, he was implacable. One square inch of dust on a table was as intolerable to him as if an entire room had been neglected. He would grab the dust cloth and redo the entire task assigned to his child. Small wonder that she gave up trying to do her household chores. They were never good enough for Dad, and he repeated them anyway, so why should she bother? In school, she carried along her own perfectionism. "If I can't be the best student in my classes, with the best grades, I just don't want to live at all," said Nan. She practiced the same implacable attitude she so resented in her father.

■ **Pushed to Excel**

James had an IQ well in the gifted range. He grasped ideas quickly and recalled them accurately. He was a bit of a daydreamer but generally could recite what had gone on in class.

Unfortunately, in his case, his parents discovered his giftedness. They wanted their son to excel, to use his genius, as they felt he could. They nagged him mercilessly. Getting an *A* minus was unacceptable. Harsh consequences and groundings grew as James, weary of their goading, gave up. He dreamed more and worked less. On many occasions, his mother would stay up late helping him complete his homework.

The teachers rarely received the fruits of those labors, though. Angry and rebellious, James refused to turn in the papers. At the end of the semester, his locker was full of them. He spent most of his time having fun. There'd be no work for James. In his early adolescent mind, doing his work would mean his parents had won. He had his pride, and he vowed to win. And win he did! But what a loss the difficult kid suffered! Only after a long hot summer in extra classes did he pass the year of school.

■ Lack of Responsibilities

In the eighth grade, Wilma was barely passing all of her courses. She tried to study and she attended classes. But she just couldn't get things together. Her pencils were not sharp, she ran out of notebook paper, and she often forgot a certain important book.

Wilma's symptoms, so annoying to her teachers, sound like a psychiatric diagnosis that is quite common. It is called attention deficit disorder (ADD), and it is treated with specific medications. It is a valid entity, but it is often misdiagnosed. In fact, I have worked with troubled children who use this familiar diagnosis as an excuse for being careless. They see it as an opportunity to avoid the laborious task of developing a sense of responsibility. Only a qualified child psychiatrist should make this diagnosis.

That, however, was not Wilma's diagnosis. As her mother and I explored the near failure of the bright girl, we discovered some important facts. Wilma had carried no responsibilities at home—ever. Even at fourteen, she had never made her bed, set the table, or washed dirty towels.

Wilma's mother grew up in a hardworking family with little income. From early morning until bedtime, she was required to be busy. At times she resented her burdened childhood, and she often vowed if she ever had children, they would be carefree and happy. They would laugh and play as she rarely had. Those children, of whom she'd dreamed, were finally there. And they did laugh and play as Mom laboriously made their beds and cleaned their rooms. How unfortunate that such well-intentioned parenting resulted in such a lazy child!

■

GUIDELINES TO AVERT LAZINESS

Laziness may be mislabeled. Many children are willing to help and want to be productive. By temperament, however, they are laid-back, relaxed individuals. Goals and achievement are not nearly as important to them as dreams and pleasurable experiences. Genuine laziness is an unwillingness to work, an active, deliberate resistance to doing known or assigned tasks.

To avoid true laziness, a child needs some well-defined guidelines:

- In preschool years, a toddler needs to have simple tasks assigned. Picking up toys at bedtime and doing errands around the house for parents are examples. He needs a parent's assistance until he shows the ability to do such tasks independently.

- Giving up total dependency and freedom is not easy. For some children, it is extremely difficult. So rewarding a child with honest praise is crucial! Mom and Dad's pride in and approval of a child's efforts make it all worthwhile.

- Increasing the responsibilities slowly, in increments, must parallel the child's development and ability. There continues to be a need for appreciation and loving approval from the adults who care for the child.

- Compliments must be honest, simple, and not gushy if they are to be believable. Be careful to compliment a child *only* when she has earned it.

- Correction and positive criticisms are vital. When praise is given for sloppy work, a child loses respect for a parent's judgment. Never hesitate to say, "I know you can do better than that. Let me know when you've finished your room the very best you can!" Then the praise will be credible.

- The laid-back child, not genuinely lazy, usually responds well to a chart or list of assigned tasks. Parents must avoid nagging but establish simple re-

wards or meaningful consequences to help such a
child.

• The manipulative child may (and often does) also
become a lazy one. Just as Brenda learned to make
her father protect her from work, so can other
forms of manipulation help keep a kid lazy. (See
chapter 7, "The Manipulative Child.")

Throughout these chapters I will remind you to be a
good role model. Teaching by example is the most convincing method I know. By working as well as playing
with your child, you will be protecting her from the ill
effects of laziness. Playing with your child can be a
highly effective means of teaching the value of being
industrious instead of lazy. And be careful to avoid over-
working, on the other end of this spectrum. A child
needs time to simply "be" as much as to "do."

The Child with a Big Mouth

5

Daryl was my kind of kid. He had rumpled sandy hair, a generously freckled face, and a rare but magic grin. He was a charming boy. So why was he in my office? Such a bright, energetic, likable ten-year-old should be out playing T-ball with his friends. What was troublesome about Daryl?

He soon let me in on his problem. "I just can't get along with my mom and dad," he stated. "They tell me I have a big mouth." Since that part of his face looked average, I knew he was alluding to his speech. As I inquired further and listened carefully, I learned some basic truths.

Daryl's version of his family went something like this. His father expected him to help with maintaining the lawn of their home. He was to weed the flower beds and trim the edges. In the fall he was to rake the leaves. Daryl loved to expend his energy in active play and hated his assigned tasks, though he knew it was only right that he should help. So help he did—but only to the accompaniment of constant complaining.

As many parents would do, Daryl's parents vigorously objected to his griping. His father often required him to repeat a particular task because he had done it carelessly. Daryl, who didn't want to do the job at all, felt doubly insulted at having to do it twice.

Some children would have pouted in silence, refusing to talk for at least the rest of the day. But not Daryl! His inborn high-energy level pressured him to express his bitter feelings loudly and repeatedly. When he had finished describing how unfair it was that he had to work so hard, he began to explain to his father that he could never please him. Dad expected everything to be impossibly perfect. Surely, he'd forgotten how boys feel. Daryl seemed driven to make Dad see his point.

You can well imagine the response of Daryl's father! No son of his would grow up lazy and careless. And he would not allow such rude and impudent talk. It took only minutes before both father and son were yelling intensely angry comments back and forth.

When it was the parents' turn to visit with me, I learned that Dad and his father had frequently had similar volatile verbal exchanges. He was passing on to his son the habits so painfully formed in his own childhood. Unless the family received help, the pattern would be repeated again with Daryl's children someday.

The bigmouthed child carries with him his habit of bluntness wherever he goes. His teachers are subjected to the stress of it as are his friends, his sports coaches, and anyone who is courageous enough to challenge or try to correct him.

Being a bigmouthed person means that individual speaks whatever thoughts occur to him. He doesn't consider the pain those words may inflict. They may be blunt or downright abusive. At the moment he is speaking, he doesn't care. He wants to make his point, get his way, or gain attention. Later, he may feel remorse or shame, but apparently, these feelings are not adequate motivators to change.

■

LIKE MOTHER, LIKE DAUGHTER

Teresa was another person whose charm and intelligence were marred by her inordinately big mouth. The harshness of her remarks infuriated her mother, outraged her teachers, and astonished her mother's friends. Though she was sixteen, old enough to know better, she regularly lost control of her words. When people asserted that she hurt their feelings, she let them know they had it coming. Sometimes she frankly stated that's just how she was and they could take it or leave it!

The story of Teresa's mother was different from that of Daryl's father. Her parents were controlling and dictatorial. She could never talk back, but she hid her painful, infuriated feelings by the power of her strong will. It was only when she had a child that she felt powerful enough to express her pent-up emotions!

Whenever she needed to correct her child, she did so vehemently. Without realizing it, she was treating Teresa very much like her parents had treated her.

As Teresa grew up, she learned how to speak up, modeling her big mouth after her mother and grandmother. All of Teresa's skills and personal charm could not neutralize the verbal abuse that she hurled at her mother. Teresa's mother had a double dose—first her mother's verbal abuse had cut her down, and now her daughter was doing much the same thing. It was difficult for the mother to understand or believe her role in Teresa's learning to use her big mouth.

THE CHILD WITH POWER

Naomi (the name I gave her) sat angrily with her mother. I observed them during the long wait between flights in an airport. She demanded popcorn, but her patient mother explained they had just finished lunch. Naomi begged, yelled, demanded, and pouted. After some twenty minutes of the abusive behavior, her mother gave in. Off they went for popcorn. After only a few handfuls, Naomi wanted no more. But she was thirsty and demanded a soda. Once again, Mom gently refused, and predictably, Naomi again became angry and abusive. This time Mother held firm, martyrishly taking a verbal beating from her daughter.

As I silently observed, I could see the pain in Mother's eyes. But to my amazement, she never corrected Naomi. In Naomi's face, I read the rapid succession of anger, confusion, guilt, and anxiety that I know so well in troubled children. Certainly, she wanted to be indulged. She was intense in her actions and reactions. But I know she needed and she wanted firm correction. Few things can be more frightening to a child than feeling more powerful than any adult in her world. Tragically, there are many such children in our world. Naomi's mom was tired. She didn't want to hurt her daughter's feelings and start an argument, so she remained silent. And Naomi's rudeness remained uncorrected. Such passivity just doesn't work!

■

REASONS FOR BIG MOUTHS

There are several reasons why children may dispense verbal abuse.

■ They Are Usually High-Energy Children

Some babies are born with the physical precursors of high energy. They experience life intensely and express themselves exuberantly. They tend to stay on the run, experience their emotions strongly, and express them with little restraint. Daryl was one of these kids.

■ They Live with One or Both Parents Who Model Verbal Abuse

Most parents don't set out to hurt their children. But sooner or later, all parents hit peaks of frustration and exhaustion that set them up to explode. When the explosions become habitual, children learn to mimic that behavior. Parents often are blind to their behaviors but feel acutely the pain of their children's retorts. They may, as did Teresa's mother, hear the excruciating echoes of their childhood in the words of their offspring.

■ Children May Get By with Rudeness without Consequences

There are many teachers of verbal abuse. From the kids next door to TV shows, rudeness in our society is expressed in every conceivable manner on a daily basis. Some parents believe they should never show impatience or demand compliance from their children. They really believe it is the *right* of children to speak and behave exactly as they choose.

These parents, by their permissiveness, allow their children to be verbally abusive. It is not the parents' poor example or their beliefs or values that are wrong—except in the area of permissiveness. They mistakenly believe that their role modeling alone will teach their children respect and good manners. Unfortunately, life rarely works that way.

■

COPING METHODS

If you are the parent of a bigmouthed child, you must be eagerly awaiting the magic wand of change. The magic comes about only through commitment and hard work. To make that work more effective and the change more rapid, you need to discover the specific cause of your child's problem. Let's consider the basic causes.

■ Gain Cooperation of the High-Energy Child

There is no way you should try to change a child's genetic heritage or personality. It's easy these days to get a doctor to prescribe medication that will alter your child's temperament, but don't yield to the temptation to overmedicate your high-energy child. For the truly hyperactive child, however, some tried and proven medications help immensely. Without altering who your child is, these medicines help her become more focused and organized. They enable her to concentrate better and lengthen her attention span.

Any medication needs to be prescribed by an experienced physician who knows your child. The physician will monitor the dosage and blood levels and will look for any problems with tolerating it. Many times, after a period of using such medicine, the child seems to develop habits and controls that allow it to be stopped. Observe your child's maturation, and ask your doctor, if you feel the time is right, to try discontinuing it.

In my experience, even more important than medication is the relationship you as a parent have with such a child. Reacting in irritation or anxiety to him will inevitably raise his anxiety level. Any indication of worry on your part will suggest to his sensitive nature that there is something seriously wrong with him. He is likely to become even more boisterous and brash to try to prove he is really okay.

On the other hand if you determine to bring such a child under your control, you are most likely to get involved in a major power struggle. Anger generates anger, and breeding of such anger wrecks relationships and prompts rebellion.

So here are my proven suggestions for you to apply:

• Keep your rules and expectations few and simple. Expecting too much on too many fronts at once dis-

courages your child. Even more important, trying to
follow through consistently in too many areas may
overwhelm you, the parent.

- Discuss your ground rules with the child. Try to explain why you feel they are necessary. Ask her if
she has a better idea for learning the lessons that
rules are intended to teach. At times she may have.
Be open to your child's ideas and incorporate them
whenever possible.
- If and when you come to agreement, write down
the rule. I recommend a bit of ceremony with child
and parents signing the contract. Post it where everyone will see it until it becomes routine.
- Make part of the agreement simple rewards and
consequences. Avoid big rewards or extended punishments. Your pride and approval are often the
best possible rewards. Express them sincerely and
regularly.
- Be friendly but firm in your follow-through. Being
angry is not a part of getting your child to respect
and obey you. Your steadfast insistence on compliance with the contract does the trick. The practice
of tough love cuts rebellion to a minimum. It allevi-
ates, at least, the temptation of a child to become a
big mouth, and it is most likely to get the desired
results.

These basic rules apply, no matter what the cause of
your child's big mouth. They are especially helpful,
however, for the high-energy, strong-willed child because they help prevent needless power struggles.

These energetic, strong-willed children respond well

to praise for their efforts to comply. Even if they complain, try to understand the heroic effort it takes for them to adapt at all. In contrast to more naturally easygoing children, the high-energy ones have to use immense willpower to give in at all. Your understanding and appreciation of your child's efforts encourage even better cooperation.

■ Recognize Family Habits

The most challenging aspect of the bigmouthed child is the parent's pride swallowing. It is easy to recognize your child's rudeness. It is equally difficult to see your own role. One father actually admitted that he did curse a little and yell at his son. "But," he protested, "I'm a man. I should be able to say what I like. When I was a kid, I had to shut up and put up with my dad's hollering. Why can't my son do the same for me?"

His was a most revealing statement. He was, indeed, taking out on his son those early frustrations of his childhood. By so intensely repeating the patterns, he was slowly and relentlessly teaching them to his son.

If you want your bigmouthed child to learn more appropriate behavior, you must show her what that behavior looks like. You'll need awareness, willpower, and determination. But be assured that you can do it. Try these methods:

- When you feel angry and start to speak harshly, take time out. Get away from the scene, breathe deeply, and make yourself think clearly.
- Remember what you want your child to do. How can she best learn the lessons that are so vital? You

· teach best by staying in control and earning a child's respect.
- When you gain control, remain firm and yet kind, focus on your child's best mode of learning, return to the scene, and deal with your child.

As you learn self-control, you will be able to teach your child to stop the flow of rude, angry words. Together, you and your child can break the family pattern of verbal abuse. And your child can replace bigmouthed behaviors with positive ones.

■ Do Not Permit Rudeness

It was primarily from her fatigue that Naomi's mother allowed the child's big mouth to function so rudely. Many parents try to correct these verbally inappropriate or even abusive children. They simply run out of energy or methods to use to stop them. Here are some ideas that you may consider:

1. At a calm moment, describe the hurts that result from your child's big mouth. Explain that other people are certain to be offended at times and that her friendships and future job may be seriously limited by her habit.
2. At some time when the child is not aware, tape a typical conversation. Later, kindly play it (privately of course) so the child himself can hear how unkind his comments sounded. Tell him you will erase or destroy the tape, and try to get an agreement that he will change his ways.
3. Develop enough confidence in yourself as the par-

ent that your child will believe you mean business. Then establish a policy that such talk will result in temporary isolation of the child in her room. You may decide on some other consequence that could be more meaningful.

4. With unerring faithfulness, follow through! If this behavior has existed unchecked for some years, it will not disappear overnight. But most bad habits can be changed in about three weeks. You can stick with anything that long.

I hope you will come to recognize that allowing a child to get by with wrong behaviors of any sort is damaging. Find the courage, seek help if you need it, and create a plan for correction. Difficult as such changes are to effect, both you and your child will be grateful that you cared enough to work it out!

6

If You'd Only Spank That Child!

Parents are often confused by the conflict in today's world regarding consequences for the misbehaviors of a young child. On the one hand, they hear of the growing menace of child abuse. They certainly don't want to be abusers. On the other hand, their older parents often say, "Mary and Jim, if you'd only spank that child, he'd learn to obey you and behave properly!"

Such predicaments come to my attention with regularity. Parents who believe administering the proverbial rod of correction means hitting children are finding out that it doesn't always work as they intend. More and more, we must look for effective and loving means of training children without hitting. As the stresses of modern living accumulate, parents are increasingly pushed to the edges of their controls. At the wrong time, with even a little extra mischief by a child, they may cross the boundary of good discipline to overpunishment or even abuse. Be aware of this possibility and you can prevent its happening.

Marvin became a difficult child because he was trained in a home that practiced abuse. His father commonly "belted" the children. Whenever Marvin or his older brother misbehaved (which was nearly every day), their father ripped off his wide heavy leather belt and applied its end to their bare buttocks. If he was *really* angry, he might use the end with the brass buckle. The brothers lived in terror of their dad's strapping, but he punished them more if they whimpered or showed fear. His sons, he vowed, would not be cowards or sissies.

Marvin learned to take his lashings stoically. He fared better than his older brother who often tried to explain to their father what he had done. Dad interpreted the efforts to explain as defiance. For that, there was still more punishment.

The brothers secretly began to take out their helpless rage on pets in the neighborhood. They caught grasshoppers and dismembered them. They became bullies at school, terrorizing younger children. Whenever he could, Marvin disobeyed his teachers and found some small sense of strength by speaking rudely to his principal, who vainly tried to correct the boy's increasing aggressiveness.

As teenagers, Marvin and his brother began to do really serious crimes. Hot-wiring cars and going joyriding became a regular source of excitement for them.

They often became involved in fights and were not permitted to ride the school bus because of their mistreatment and bullying of other students. But they didn't really care because they didn't like school anyway. It was boring. Besides, if they did make good grades, their dad might believe their success was to his credit because he applied "strict" rules and heavy punishments. They resented him so much, they couldn't bear his believing that his harshness was working.

These boys will be extremely good candidates for the performance of major crime in the future. Inwardly terrified, but outwardly calloused, they are learning to live on the edge—playing adult games of cops and robbers. They found they could get by with really serious behaviors much of the time. At heart, they believed their conduct would prove, to Dad and to their own frightened selves, that they were not cowards. They were as powerful as their tyrannical father!

When I knew this young man (and so many similar ones), he could tell me of only minor misbehaviors as a small child. He said that he came to believe his father found pleasure in hitting him and his brother.

When such events are reported to a child abuse agency, it is common that definitive help cannot be found. The parents learn to bluster their way out of any corrective action. Furthermore, they terrify their children even more by threatening them if they report abuse. These abused children will no longer reveal the brutality in their homes.

You may believe such an extreme example of creating a difficult child is rare. Let me assure you it is not. Throughout our country, prisons are full of people who have entered into crime as a displacement of their rage and anguish from abusive parents onto others. Newspaper columns and TV shows reveal the dramatic stories of damaged people every day. More and more of them are children or adolescents.

But how about concerned and conscientious parents who firmly believe that sparing the rod spoils the child? They recognize that spanking their child has not effected the change that's needed. What else can be done? On the other extreme, parents are often intimidated by the fear of being reported to authorities if they punish a wayward child. They feel they should be spanking their child.

Common sense and clearly established goals can help you out of this dilemma:

- Consider your temperament and that of your child. Could you lose control and punish too severely? Does your child respond favorably to physical punishment by changing her misbehaviors?
- Focus clearly on the lesson your child needs to learn. What is the least severe discipline that will effectively teach that lesson?
- Remember the motto, "True strength is always gentle, and real gentleness is always strong." (I don't know who stated it, but it's so true!) Practice that philosophy.

To spank or not to spank is *not* the issue! How to raise healthy, godly, and productive children with love is the challenge. Read on.

RISKY BEHAVIOR

Let's focus our interest now on a child who was mismanaged in another way.

Anne was always an energetic child. As an infant, she cried loudly, and quieting her took some time. When she reached the age of two, she could climb from the floor to a chair to the stove top to the cupboards to the top of the refrigerator. With her prowess, cookies were never off-limits to her. She could also get to the medicine cupboard atop the bathroom sink. It was not uncommon for her to test a variety of pills stored in that cupboard. Anne became a frequent visitor to the local emergency room and clinics.

At last it was my turn to restrain the child, insert a tube into her tummy, and remove the potentially fatal pills. When I learned that it was the sixth time in two weeks for the painful procedure to take place, Anne's mother and I had a long talk. The conversation likely saved the child's life.

The mother, you see, was quite the opposite of Marvin's father. She was a happy-go-lucky person who reacted impulsively to Anne's skirmishes with danger. She collected her off the top of the refrigerator and told her —with a grin—not to climb up there again. Later, Anne overheard Mom telling Grandma about her accomplishments, and it sounded to Anne as if she had done something wonderful and cute. Her bright mind would quickly think up more escapades.

With her Sunday school teachers and with her sitter,

Anne was an undisciplined, incorrigible child. It took two people to keep her in tow because she seemed to be everywhere and nowhere. She recognized no boundaries and knew no authority.

Anne's troublesome behavior was annoying most people around her, exhausting her mother, and endangering her very life. She was getting into more risky behaviors almost daily.

Between the extremes of Marvin and Anne, there is a successful middle-of-the-road sort of correction that works. Marvin and his brothers rebelled against the excessive anger and punishment of their dad. Anne was allowed so much freedom, she abused it to the point of risking her very life.

Learning how to establish rules and define a child's boundaries clearly is the beginning of good training. Maintaining these limits and enforcing the rules consistently are the next steps. Using methods that are individually worked out to fit each child's personality will complete a plan that will prevent many difficulties for both child and parent. Let me remind you, the least angry and severe a method *that gets results* is obviously the best to use.

■

ROWDY BEHAVIOR

Twenty-two-month-old Bert minds his mother—at times. Many more times, she related, he refuses to cooperate and yells, "No!" when she asks him to do something. Her question is this: "How can I correct Bert? Should I spank him or put him in time-out?"

Of course, Bert refused to sit still in time-out. By the time I knew his mother, he had become immune to her spankings. He was literally running the household. She was correct when she commented, "Dr. Grace, I think he's smarter than I am."

Bert is very likely to become a difficult child if his mother continues to feel helpless, changes her rules and consequences, and gives in to him. Is spanking the answer?

■
REACTIVE BEHAVIOR

Here is another mother's predicament: "My little boy gets mad when I spank him or when he has to stop doing things he likes to do. He will try to hit and kick me or the person who corrects him."

As I've explained earlier, spanking or other physical punishment doesn't work for some children. In fact, it carries some risk of crossing the line into abuse. Daily, abused children end up in emergency rooms. Regularly, children die from overpunishment. And the hidden damage to a child's spirit from excessive punishment is immeasurable.

■
THE WAY TO CORRECTION

My advice, opening me to criticism, must increasingly be this: do not hit your child to correct him. "If you'd only spank that child" is not sound advice. Neither, of course, is it a good practice to overindulge or pamper a child.

How can the parents of all the Berts, Annes, and Marvins of our world correct their youngsters? How can a parent prevent the development of a difficult child in the family? If spanking creates or worsens the problem, having a time-out doesn't work, and speaking sternly frightens a child, what's a parent to do?

Here are some specific guidelines.

■ Know Yourself

How strong is your self-control? Is it possible, even with the best intentions, that you could spank too hard? How would you feel later if you realized you had left bruises on your child's body? Even worse, how about scars on her spirit?

■ Never Correct a Child in the Heat of Your Anger

These words, so wisely taught and practiced by my mother, are profoundly true. I urge you to seek methods other than spanking, but infinitely more important than your method of correction is the intensity of your anger toward your child. Gain control of your emotions before you begin to deal with your child. You probably need to take time out to think. If your child is under three, don't take too much time. A toddler may forget in a short time what he did that was wrong.

■ Know Your Child

Each child has a unique set of personality traits. Some youngsters can be corrected effectively by a gentle touch or glance. Others require immense energy and persistence to learn to respect parental authority.

■ Use the Least Severe Consequences that Will Teach the Lesson

When you overpunish a sensitive child, the result is likely to be a wounded spirit. When you do so to a strong-willed child, the result is often rebellion. Do you see why you need to know your child? The prevention of rearing a problem child depends on it. A toddler may need only firm restraint and a stern look and voice; a school-age child needs consequences; an adolescent usually respects the time-honored punishment of grounding.

■ The Worst of All Corrective Actions Is None at All!

Permissiveness means to a child that his parents do not care about him or that they are powerless. Do correct your child with one or more of these successful means:

- State clearly and firmly what rule your child has broken. This means that you have established your basic family policies.
- Ask your child what she is willing to do to correct the misbehaviors. Give her time to think and to choose wisely.
- Stop the child's world until he obeys, practicing that good choice.
- Effectively correcting a child is neither easy nor convenient. If she has to miss an important event or

suffer some other consequence to help her learn a lifelong lesson, your efforts will be well worth it!

Correcting a difficult child is an ongoing challenge. It demands individualizing, being persistent, and exercising wisdom and creativity and tough love. To prevent serious rebellion and build godly character demands all these qualities as well as time and energy. God loves your child even more than you do. He loves you, too, and will guide and empower you in this crucial task.

7

The Manipulative Child

"I have a headache, Daddy. I just can't do the dishes today!" Somehow I managed to fix a woebegone expression on my face that convinced my skeptical father. I knew there were other children who could do those horrible dishes, so no one was really the worse for my half-true complaints. The dishes were done, and I was able to lie down, nurse my aches, and read my precious book.

A few days later, I managed to work up another painful head. Once again my father looked at my face and agreed I could get out of the onerous duty of dishwashing. That time, however, he wasn't so easy. He said, "Gracie, if your head hurts too bad to wash dishes, I'm certain it hurts too much to read. You'll just have to go to bed and sleep it away."

That was not what I had in mind. But I knew my father. His decision was final, and his word was the law! I did go to bed, without my book, spending a boring summer afternoon alone. I learned quickly that trying to manipulate my parents by playing sick just wouldn't work.

My dad's careful observations and tough love taught me early in life that manipulations didn't work. I was a fortunate child.

Perhaps you know people who have become master manipulators. Folks you work with (or even live with) may manipulate you every day. You finally come to resent them, feeling tricked by them. Their problems began in childhood, and they were clearly difficult even then!

■

DARREN'S TRICKERY

Let me explain. Darren was a manipulator whose parents failed to discern what he did. When it was his bedtime, he feigned immense terror. His mother experienced horrifying nightmares as a child, so she readily believed he was afraid. Only after she lay in bed cuddling him would he get quiet. It took only a moment, and he was smiling and enjoying her company. She was allowing him to take control of her time and permitting him to be dishonest and selfish.

Had he been truly frightened, he would not have recovered so quickly. He would have awakened during the night with frightening dreams. And her presence near him with a dim light and soothing music for a brief time would generally have comforted him.

With his father, Darren mastered a different trick. Dad worked long hours and often arrived home just at his son's bedtime. Truly delighted to see his dad, Darren would cling to him and tell him how much he had missed him. He would beg for at least one story. But one was never enough. He "needed" Daddy to read just one more book or create one more Darren story. Daddy, you see, felt more than a little guilty for being away so much. He loved his son and was flattered by Darren's wishes for "just one more." He could even brag to his friends about the loving relationship he enjoyed with his son.

But Darren's dad, like his mom, failed to see beneath the surface. They allowed their experiences to make them believe Darren was sincere. And they unconsciously let their emotions of remembered fears and present guilt rule their actions.

It was a compliment to Darren's parents that he craved time with them. His seeking more time with Dad to compensate for those long hours was natural. Both parents needed to give him time, attention, and comfort. The problem was that they gave too much, allowing Darren to be the boss. They did so out of trying to meet their own need to feel they were good parents rather than recognizing Darren's need for some limits.

Over time, they all paid a high, negative price for their deceptions. Both parents came to resent the tyranny that grew imperceptibly but relentlessly in Darren. His power to control their time and demand their every attention robbed them of time for each other and for themselves. Each began to accuse the other of spoiling the boy, and they regularly had heated exchanges over the daily events.

Darren felt guilty about his deceptions, but he enjoyed the power and attentions too much to give up his trickery. When he practiced his well-developed prowess on his classmates, they hated it, but due to his learned charm, they, too, fell under the spell of his power. When his teachers complained about his manipulations, he would cry out to his indulgent parents. Remembering the harshness of teachers from their past, they identified with "poor Darren." His control was nearly complete. Parents, friends, teachers—all performed his bidding.

■

THE ULTIMATE THREAT

A teacher wrote of her concern about a manipulative preadolescent youngster: "How should I respond to a child who says she wants to die? She hurts herself in small ways and uses these hurts to get attention. How can I balance care and concern with avoiding such manipulative behaviors?"

Children are uncanny in their ability to sense their parents' and teachers' vulnerable spots. In some cases, being hateful overpowers sensitive parents. In others, it may be a threat to run away. But in all too many homes and classrooms, young people threaten a permanent "solution" to their problems—suicide. These young people see threatening suicide as a way out of responsibilities or punishment. They truly think about it, but most of those with whom I have worked say they really never wanted to die. They wanted someone to pay attention to them, and they discovered the threats worked. Furthermore, they often were relieved of onerous duties, and they learned that their parents treated them with the proverbial kid gloves—for a time.

Please remember that many young people do find life hopeless. They feel helpless and fear things will never get better. Their threats are serious and demand professional help and treatment. In chapter 16, you'll find the signs of serious suicidal intent and the steps to take toward help.

After a while, of course, the adults begin to catch on to the manipulative aspect of suicidal threats. They quit paying attention and resume their old habits, and the child resorts to more serious threats and begins self-damaging acts. He may take a handful of aspirin or scratch superficially on his wrists with the end of a paper clip or even a razor blade. Occasionally, and tragically, a young person "accidentally" dies from a wrongly calculated overdose. The person on whom he had relied to discover him failed to show up.

■
THE SNEAKY MANIPULATOR

Yet another type of manipulation came to my attention from a mother's question. "What about the sneaky, compliant child?" she wrote. "How can I deal with him?" Her twelve-year-old son, Brandon, was a model child—on the surface. It was his nine-year-old sister who yelled and fought. With great frequency she had to endure punishments for her aggressive behaviors.

One day, however, Mom happened to enter the room unbeknownst to the two children. She saw her son poke his sister hurtfully. Then Mom heard him taunt the little girl with the epithet "Tattletale!" No wonder she yelled and attacked him! That "model" son was actually manipulative—he hurt his sister and created an unhealthy environment for the entire family by allowing her to take the blame when she exploded at him.

CURBING MANIPULATIVE BEHAVIOR

There are various expressions of manipulation, and each is hurtful. Teach your child to avoid this practice. Here are some guidelines to help you.

■ Be Aware

The sweetest child may learn how to get out of work, get her way, or get a competing sibling into trouble by being basically dishonest.

■ Search Your Values and Habits

Not everyone agrees that manipulation is an undesirable practice. Although manipulation is common, it is a form of profound dishonesty. If you see its harmful effects, you will be more likely to put energy into curbing this practice in your child.

■ Teach Your Child

My father did not hit me or shame me in teaching me to stop cheating my way out of my duties. He required me to function properly, no matter what my excuses were. You, too, may teach your child that such dishonesty is not okay and that it won't work out.

■ Be Observant

Brandon's mother eventually caught his tormenting of his sister by accident. Perhaps if she had been more observant, she could have corrected his behavior earlier.

■ Be Consistent

The importance of follow-through cannot be overemphasized. You may have the best ideas in the world; you may catch your child now and then and correct her occasionally. But if you let manipulative habits go uncorrected even once in a while, your child will try harder to get by another time.

Tempting as it may be to deal with people, including your family, through manipulative techniques, don't do it! And be alert to the likelihood your child will attempt this art. If he gets by with it, he will finally develop the habit that keeps others guessing what he *really* means and what may be the hidden agenda. A child with such a habit is indeed a difficult child. Teach, model, and require absolute honesty and forthrightness. With these qualities, family life becomes much easier and more comfortable.

8

That Silly Child!

Matt could always make the family laugh. Whether the situation was light or tense, he found the humor and reflected it for everyone to enjoy. Many times major conflicts were averted through Matt's apparent gift of humor.

Matt was a stocky young man when I knew him. He wore his visored cap backward, and the bill kept bumping into the back of his chair, knocking it askew. Matt kept busy straightening his cap, and more than once I had difficulty focusing on the problems that prompted the visit with me. He was in no way perturbed, however, and grinned his way through our visit.

As I became acquainted with Matt, I learned that he was unable to participate in the spring track events because his grades were below the minimum requirements. He would not be able to compete for a coveted spot on the swim team or on the football team because of his academic deficiencies.

When I looked for some telltale sign of remorse on Matt's face, I couldn't find one. I felt sad over his losses; but he assured me that it was okay. He could do all those things next year. He was perfectly happy with his life. He'd rather have fun anyway, and sports had lots of restrictions. He was full of anecdotes and funny stories. But he never got around to telling me about losing a near relative in death. He failed to mention an illness that threatened the life of a grandparent.

Matt did tell me, however, another piece of useful information. Many times he faced severe consequences for his failures. For example, his parents would ground him until there was solid evidence of better grades. Good-naturedly, he accepted the grounding. "In fact," he said with a grin, "I knew it would help me study if I stayed at home off the phone."

Picking up on the grin, I asked him to tell me the longest time he was grounded. The usual time was from one to three weeks. But the longest grounding he actually served, Matt stated, with another wide smile, was only two or three days. Matt believed his parents were highly gullible and too easy on him. And so they were! But he failed to recognize the problem that had invaded his charming personality.

It is true of many personal traits that one's greatest asset can become the gravest liability. That's what happened with Matt's delightful humor. He had stumbled onto the realization that he could use it to charm everyone. He could get project deadlines extended and groundings abbreviated. He could get by with rudeness, even verbal cruelty, by couching his comments in a cover of humor.

The humor gone awry had resulted in serious damage to Matt himself. The playfulness that had seemed so harmless rebounded, narrowing Matt's boundaries and limiting the goals he really was pursuing.

SILLINESS TO OVERCOME STRESS

Audrey wrote about her "silly" child. Alice took nothing seriously. The saddest TV shows could always make her laugh, and the most stringent consequences meant nothing to her. Not only did she consistently giggle, but she seemed to care nothing about her responsibilities. Avoiding her duties was a challenge, and since disciplinary action was equally meaningless to her, she sailed through her days carefree.

The question Audrey asked was perceptive: "Do children resort to being silly to overcome stressful situations?" Her daughter had grown up through some difficulties. Various illnesses and financial stresses had caused worry and tension in the family. Alice had been aware of her parents' distress and sensed that they took it out on each other and the children at times. Audrey also knew that Alice was a sensitive child, overly reactive to issues of concern.

Audrey was absolutely right. The silliness that was not only annoying but also worrisome was a cover-up for anxiety resulting from stress. The child's response to pain had become the habit of laughing it off.

Perhaps to a degree, that reaction is almost universal. When I stumbled and fell on a stairway in front of several people, they all giggled. Yet several offered to help me up. After dusting off myself and collecting my dignity, I recalled similar circumstances in which I, too, had laughed at someone's calamity. Not once had I felt happy about the person's distress. I was anxious, unwilling to cry in public, and trying to express some emotion, I turned to gallows humor. Gallows humor is the dark laughter that tries to make light of potentially fatal problems.

No matter how well one understands such perverse humor, it is harmful. As the victim of laughter at my expense, I knew the embarrassment and helplessness I felt. As a perpetrator on other occasions, I knew equally well that no one intended to harm my pride by laughing.

Silliness is an expression of tension, and it is also a way to relieve pressure. Alice was overwhelmed by the many concerns of her family. She had discovered a measure of relief through giggling under duress. Her silliness even brought, at times, a smile to the worried faces of her parents. And so her habit grew, becoming eventually like the proverbial weed—a plant out of place, a sense of humor out of control.

The harmful effects of the silly child are evident in all areas of life. In restaurants, I have observed customers' looks of offense as they believe they are being ridiculed by giggling kids. In school, classrooms can become places of uproar when even one silly child infects those around him. At home, such giddiness can make parents feel helpless and angry. Among friends, silliness may seem fun, and it is temporarily contagious. But very commonly the end result is lack of respect for the airhead the silly person seems to be.

We need to distinguish harmful silliness from healthy good humor. Nearly everyone understands the benefits of the latter. But it can be difficult to tell where the line is that separates one from the other. Healthy good humor is that relating to something ludicrous, absurd, and comical. It avoids hurting others and is not usually annoying. Unhealthy dark humor often seems comical, but it emanates from fear and anger, as in Alice, or an effort to manipulate, like Matt did. It confuses and annoys people who hear it. Commonly, it becomes abusive when it includes a subtle attack on another person.

When silly kids grow up, they usually become equally silly adults. If silliness involves a cynical aspect, based on anger, it is almost certain to result in emotional abuse. What one learns as a child, if uncorrected, becomes an adult habit and thus the cycle is perpetuated from parent to child to grandchild.

■

HOW TO ALLEVIATE SILLINESS

If you have a young child who seems to be headed in the direction of extreme and hurtful silliness, act at once. Encourage healthy, positive laughter, humor that is at the expense of no one. Healthy humor never hurts another person or group. It is not present during obvious tragedy or during another's pain or embarrassment. It does not disguise heartache or danger, even risking the failure to address issues or solve problems.

Healthy laughter does relieve tension; it avoids the exaggeration of stress and prevents habits of seeing doom and feeling pessimistic. Laugh with your child, and practice searching for appropriate humor in all of the situations where it exists. But don't use laughter to avoid dealing with pain or to hurt another person.

Perhaps your child already exhibits signs of excessive silliness. To make matters more complicated, you may have become irritated at his habit. Due to your frustration, you are likely to react to his giddiness by demanding that your child stop it. You possibly have expressed deep concern at the seeming lack of compassion for others.

But think for a moment about the dynamics just explained. If your child is acting silly to avoid pain and relieve tension, what will your demands or disapproval do? Instead of motivating your child to change, your response will create more tension. Your child will likely giggle more, adding to your irritation. The development of one of the vicious circles of life is probable.

■ Talk About It

So why not try a different approach? Here is a possible dialogue.

"Danny, I noticed how you laughed when your friend Kurt fell during your ball game today. I saw the hurt look on his face. I don't believe you enjoy seeing people get hurt. So I'm wondering if you laughed because you were afraid he could be hurt, and you didn't want to cry. Were you worried about Kurt? Or maybe you could see yourself in his place. Were you afraid you might fall sometime?"

It's wise to await an answer when talking with a child. Danny could respond, "Gosh! Dad, I never even thought about it. It was kind of mean to laugh at Kurt's fall. Yeah, I did feel kinda nervous, and that laugh just slipped out!"

If you, the parent, have spoken kindly with a genuine wish to help your child break a bad habit, she is likely to react similarly to Danny. Then you are free to suggest, "Next time you feel nervous, what might you do?"

Often, children think of excellent possibilities. Danny may decide to use his energy to run and help his friend get up. He could let his concern show and ask if Kurt is okay. Or he could say to his friend, "I'm so sorry you fell. I was afraid you had sprained your ankle!"

Putting real, bottom-line emotions into clear, honestly stated words is the best possible means of preventing excessive silliness. Practicing these communication skills will also alleviate it.

■ Teach Healthy Feelings

During television programs that portray tragedy, you can teach healthy feelings. If your child, like Alice, laughs at a drama of pain, take advantage of the commercial breaks, or reserve talking time at the end. Without lecturing, stimulate an in-depth conversation about the program. Ask leading questions: "How do you think you would have handled that tough situation?" "I was feeling really frightened when the robber climbed in that window. I don't know how I would have handled it!" Admitting your adult vulnerability can give your child permission to admit her uncertainty and anxiety. And when fears are out in the open, they usually lose their immensity. Issues and problems that stimulate such vulnerable emotions are almost always solvable.

There is always the potential for good in a negative quality, and conversely, negatives are commonly found in good situations. This principle is remarkably true in the case of humor. As has been stated, good humor enhances health and lightens the burdens of life. But humor gone awry not only fails to provide these positives, it often becomes malicious. It can become, in fact, a means of abusing others.

If you as a parent have such a habit, developed perhaps without your realizing it, break it. If you recognize this habit in your child, teach him how hurtful it is, and help him change. Transform negative humor into positive through the methods and insights you've read about. You will thus eliminate one more of the difficulties affecting the life of your child.

The Deceitful Child

9

"I just can't stand being lied to!" Mike roared. His troubled gray eyes were glaring, and his entire demeanor reflected the anger he felt. "Four times this week," he continued, "Tom has deceived me!" He went on to list the various categories of Tom's deceit. They included unfinished school projects, neglected household responsibilities, disregarded curfews, and a list of half-truths that had finally been uncovered.

Mike's lifelong practice of absolute honesty held high priority on his list of values. It's small wonder that he felt so betrayed, so hurt by the adolescent son he had tried to teach.

Tom carefully glued his gaze to the carpet on which his size thirteens rested. At least he had the grace to feel ashamed of his behaviors. As is so often the case, even a veteran liar can sometimes be honest about lies. "Yes,"

Tom admitted, "I don't always tell the truth. It's just not in my best interest to do that!"

Further discussion revealed the history of Tom's problem and the deceit that caused it. Both of his parents worked and were extremely busy. Their short weekends and brief evenings at home did not provide the time to follow through with the requirements of effective training of their children.

They created fairly good policies for the family. Responsibilities were fair and evenly parceled out among their three children. Mom and Dad certainly did their share of the work, even though much of that was done while the kids slept.

As a second child, Tom was easygoing and, frankly, lazy. He'd rather play video games or go swimming with his buddies than clean the garage. His messy room, he claimed, was the way he liked it. Early on, he had learned to stuff all of the clutter in his room under the bed. His mother's hasty checkout tolerated Tom's sloppy work. He'd been able to get off. He got out of cleaning the garage by bribing his younger sister to do it. Out of his allowance, he saved just enough to pay her to pick up the trash and make the garage look superficially okay.

The more Tom's lies and deceptions worked, the more he employed them. Once in a while he was caught and had to pay the price of extra work, lectures, and grounding. But the great majority of the time, he'd gotten by. Lying seemed to work. Life was so much easier because of the growing habit.

His teachers and coach discovered that he had cheated

on exams and lied about keeping the rules of the team. His girlfriend found she could not trust his word or his actions. The natural consequences of Tom's deceit were slowly tightening the net about him. His father discovered several unpaid speeding tickets. A number of school reports, undelivered, were located in his room, which his desperate mother finally cleaned. The speedometer on the car spoke its silent testimony to trips Tom had been denied but had sneaked out and taken anyway.

The evidence was too strong to ignore, and Tom and his parents sought help. They accepted that a destructive habit has no simple cause and that changing it is both complex and grueling. Nevertheless, tough love won and Tom learned healthier habits.

Here are some of the steps through which Tom's family laboriously struggled:

- Tom had enough integrity to admit that *he* had a problem. His parents were wise in refusing to take the responsibility for his troublesome habit. And Tom was genuinely remorseful.
- Tom's parents did see, however, that their trust had crossed the line into gullibility. They had failed to check out and follow through as thoroughly as they should have.
- Realizing trust in their son had been betrayed, Mike and his wife, Sue, formulated some criteria for rebuilding that lost trust. They would wait up for him to come home and personally check his schoolwork and call his teachers.
- Because Tom loved his parents, he agreed to their

tight stipulations, and he was willing to accept both the limits and the consequences.

In his thought-provoking book *People of the Lie*, Dr. M. Scott Peck described the frightening end point of deceit. It is possible, he wrote, for people to practice dishonesty so long and so intently that they cross an invisible line. They can so forcefully rationalize and deny the truth that they lose the capacity to distinguish truth from lies.

Mike was well advised to take his son's habit seriously. His tough love protected his son from crossing that treacherous line.

■

DECEIT BEYOND CHILDHOOD

K ent and Kelley were parents of an only child. She was diminutive, quiet, and compliant. As a child, she easily passed for several years younger than she actually was. Long after she crossed the chronological dividing line between child and student rates, her parents got by with the kids' prices on tickets and in restaurants. Meg eventually realized that her friends' parents did not rely on those dishonest practices.

She caught on to her father's collecting certain fees in his business in cash. She discovered that he managed his records to avoid paying income taxes on some of that money. When certain people called her father on the phone, she was instructed to state that he was not at home.

When Meg reached adolescence, she started concocting lies to tell her parents. She had been well taught in ways to evade responsibilities and consequences. She made up stories about where she was going and with whom. She cleverly enlisted the help of her friends to carry out her deceit to a "successful" conclusion. Meg could get around the rules of life just as her parents had wordlessly taught her.

It was only after she was married that Meg finally stopped her habits. When her husband discovered her constant lies, he gave her an ultimatum—either become honest or learn to live without him. He could not handle her deception. With help and heroic efforts, Meg did change her practices. Old habits, so deeply rooted in early childhood, were most difficult to break. Again and again she backslid. But their love and commitment enabled them to stick it out. Recently, her husband stated, "I have reasonable hope that we're going to make it. Several times lately, I've checked and found that Meg is finally being honest."

A serious problem such as deceit rarely, if ever, develops suddenly in a child. By parents' active practices or disregard of the symptoms, a child's problems are related to those of her parents. One of the immeasurably big challenges of parenting is to find and walk the line—the fine line of their part in a child's problems and insistence on that child's facing her own part.

Meg did not have the blessing of her parents' honesty in accepting their defective examples. They never admitted their role in forming her habit of deceit. She had to overcome the problem without their help. Her loving and committed husband paid much of the price for the parents' wrongdoing. Nevertheless, together Meg and her husband will prevail. And I suspect their children will learn honesty from the cradle!

A WIDESPREAD TREND

If you are a parent who has not learned Meg's lessons, I hope this book will awaken you. For decades, our Western culture, and much of the world, has distorted values. Instead of walking the line of honesty with integrity, a great many people have perceived their goal in life to be getting away with as much deceit as possible. They raise retail prices for all of us by shocking amounts of shoplifting. Tools and supplies on the job "walk away" on the bodies of employees. These robbers raise prices on goods and services because their companies include this huge cost in increased prices. Efforts to stop such deplorable practices seem to have given way to complacent permission by society as long as someone pays.

With such permissive attitudes around them, parents may yield to the temptation to be lax in their value of honesty. It is easy then to overlook deceit and dishonesty in their children. Preventing or remedying these habits requires consistent effort, and the motivation that prompts such effort demands total conviction that deception is wrong.

It is frightening to catch glimpses of a world filled with difficult kids who have grown to adulthood with their problems intensified. When people of sound morals see the apparent fringe benefits of lying, cheating, and stealing, it is tempting for them to feel they, too, should reap those benefits.

■
HEALTHY MORALS

Deceit is only one example of pathological moral development. Biblical teachings, for the Judeo-Christian world, stand unsurpassed in conveying positive moral principles.

These ancient laws are noted in Exodus 20:3–17 and repeated in Deuteronomy 5:7–21. Simply stated, these are the ten laws undergirding all of our complex legal system:

1. "You shall have no other gods before Me."
2. "You shall not make for yourself a carved image [an idol to worship]."
3. "You shall not take the name of the LORD your God in vain [or speak lightly or derogatorily of God]."
4. "Remember the Sabbath day, to keep it holy."
5. "Honor your father and your mother." (This is unconditional.)
6. "You shall not murder."
7. "You shall not commit adultery."
8. "You shall not steal."
9. "You shall not bear false witness against your neighbor."
10. "You shall not covet your neighbor's house; you shall not covet your neighbor's wife, nor his male servant, nor his female servant, . . . nor anything that is your neighbor's."

These laws are full of power. What a wonderful world we would all enjoy if they were kept!

■

SOME STAGES OF MORAL DEVELOPMENT

As simple as these ten laws are, the moral strength to follow them takes some development. And teaching this exercise is the privilege of good parents.

■ Infancy

Moral development begins with the foundation of trust that loving parents build in tiny babies. When infants are secure in having their needs met by faithful, mature parents, they become bonded or attached to those people. Because of mutual love, each gives in to the other some of their will and wishes. At first all the giving is from parents, but gradually, the child learns to give up some of her wishes. The growing respect and love this creates are the rewards for giving up the all-consuming early wish of an infant to control, be utterly selfish, and be totally cared for.

The foundation for teaching honesty begins with parents proving themselves to be trustworthy. The credible love of parents breeds love and security in a baby, and the strength of these qualities enables a child to give up his selfish will.

■ Early Childhood (Preschool)

By finding their infant needs met in comforting and loving ways, babies increase their trust and love for their families. By God's design as well as by their natural, healthy development, toddlers begin to separate from the adults in their lives. They often resist parents' authority and try out their own power. They are, of course, in no way ready to control their lives, let alone their households. But two-year-olds rightly explore how far they can go in asserting their individuality and independence. Wise parents encourage this push for autonomy, but they balance it with clear, protective boundaries.

The crucial lessons for two-year-olds require these steps for mastery:

- They must explore their geographic and behavioral environments. Parents need to provide an environment for play that is challenging but safe. They need to be within easy sight and hearing of the child at all times to provide that safety.
- They must recognize their boundaries and learn to live within them, even when no one can see. A stern "No!" and firm restraint must be used most consistently if a child is to respect the established limits. This step is the most important one I know in gaining respect for authority.
- A meaningful consequence must be applied every time a toddler oversteps her boundaries. Time-out for two or three minutes, or firm restraint by the parent if she refuses to sit still in time-out, is my favorite consequence for a child of this age.
- Constant vigilance by the parent is necessary to provide the follow-through required to finish this procedure.
- Every time a toddler does give up some of her will

or her desires in order to obey and respect her parents, she deserves praise: "Tina, I know you hated to stop playing and pick up your toys, but you did it! I'm very proud of you!"

When these steps have been followed consistently over several weeks, toddlers will begin to add to their earlier trust the essential respect for authority and the bending of their will in learning compliance. Now they are ready for the growth in creativity and independence of ages three and four.

By the age of three or four, children recognize that misbehaviors often result in unpleasant, if not downright painful, consequences. They do what is right because they are respectful of those results more than because they really know the best or care to do it. Parents, you can readily see, will achieve these healthy behavioral habits by having the clear steps established you have just finished reading about and enforcing them consistently. It is not necessary to hit children to ensure their obedience. Firmness and follow-through with prearranged consequences teach adequately.

By age three—and even earlier—children usually listen to reason, and explanations go a long way toward gaining obedience and proper behavior. As children mature, they begin to see that their good behaviors make life better for them. To their surprise, they discover life is better for their parents and others, too. So they add to their awareness of consequences, good or bad, the fact that everyone gets along better when family values are practiced.

■ Late Childhood

By the age of twelve, more or less, children have learned that compliance and generally good behaviors gain for them the approval of others. Since one of our basic emotional needs is this very quality of pride and approval from others, this stage of development is most important. It is crucial that parents, teachers, and other adults express their pleasure in children's efforts as well as success in achieving good behaviors.

Between the ages of six and twelve, children should learn to be responsible. If the sense of respect and obedience based on trust and love is well established (as explained earlier), responsibility can be achieved fairly easily. These insights will help you reach this goal with your child:

- Responsibility is gained through a child's ability to make wise decisions. Developing this skill demands that parents give the child limited choices as often as possible. Help her gather information about each choice, and then allow her to decide. Certainly, you won't give her freedom to choose any issue that would put her at serious risk. But freedom to make many decisions offers two benefits to a child. Wise choices enable parents and teachers to point out her skills and compliment her, building self-esteem. Poor decisions can be used to teach what was wrong and facilitate better choices next time.

- Reminding a child of tasks does not help him become responsible. In fact, it often teaches him to rely on his parent's responsibility. It works far more effectively to allow the natural consequences of ir-responsibility to be the child's teachers.

- Avoid any angry "I told you so, Dummy!" remarks. Rubbing the child's proverbial face in the mess of a poor choice is more likely to result in rebellion or depression than in responsibility.

- A child needs to endure some pain from the consequences of poor choices if she is to learn the necessary lessons. So *avoid rescuing her.* Encourage her and help her do better next time, but don't try to remove the discomfort that motivates growth.

■ Adolescence

Still later, in adolescence, young people learn that their world works best when they do their duty, respect authority, and maintain the lawful social order. They choose or reject moral or religious teachings and beliefs during their teens.

Many thoughtful adolescents understand that right and wrong are social terms affecting not just them but the world around them. Life can be seen, then, as related to community welfare and to universal human right.

Adolescents learn best by parents' guiding their thinking. Ask them honestly thoughtful questions about their ideas and proposed plans. Help them discover how to live safely as well as successfully. More learning will happen if they discover the consequences of their choices without parents rescuing them. Nevertheless, parents will need to add some of their own consequences to the natural ones. Losing privileges, being grounded, and losing an allowance are good examples. Be careful to avoid belittling teenagers, and don't bring up old mistakes. Help them learn from each event, and let them move on.

■ Adulthood

The peak of moral development is the commitment to belief in the sacredness of life, showing one's inner certainty that sharing mutual respect and regard for oneself and others is the capstone of good living.

If you can teach and exemplify these steps to healthy morality, your child is most likely to avoid being deceitful!

10
The Too Good Child

Her face was far too worried for a twelve-year-old! Big tears welled up in her eyes, overflowed, and dripped on her flowered tee shirt. Beth had been relating to me the list of concerns that disturbed her sleep and distracted her mind daily.

What if Dad lost his job? She had overheard talk between her parents that sounded as if he might. And Mom hadn't taken it well when he was talking about work. It almost sounded as if they might get a divorce. Her best friend's parents had separated only a few weeks before. Dad complained about the house a lot, and it was a mess. She had spent hours trying to pick up and dust, but she couldn't make it good enough. Her brother was not helping. His grades were not very good, and their parents scolded him almost every day. He'd begun yelling back at them. Beth studied as hard as she could, hoping to make it up to her parents.

Even Beth's appearance pictured the good child she was. Her black hair glistened, and her clothes were neatly pressed and clean. Her fingernails, bitten to the quick, were clean, and her pink cheeks had been well scrubbed. Her speech was soft and her words, well chosen. Despite her worries, Beth meticulously avoided any hint of disloyalty to or criticism of her family.

Beth, at first look, seemed to be a child who did not need to be in the office of a psychiatrist. But under her blanket of extreme goodness was an amazing cluster of problems. Her transparent face pictured both sadness and fear. Her bitten fingernails were evidence of anxiety, and her description of personal and family problems was convincing.

In many families, there is a Beth, a child who learns how to be too good. But that goodness can become harmful, resulting in emotional illness.

■

A SERIOUS BUSINESS

Damon was another too good child. Nine-year-old Damon would sit quietly at his desk all morning, hardly moving except for his eyes that pursued the pages of work he was assigned. With twenty-seven other students, many severely misbehaving, Mrs. Jones was only too happy about Damon.

As the year wore on, she began to realize that Damon's work was always perfect. There were many careful erasures, but the final appearance of those papers was meticulous. He never disobeyed class rules. At play, he was serious, always careful to avoid hurting playmates, and he was intent on getting it exactly right.

Mrs. Jones's many commendations rarely caused a smile to cross Damon's sober face. Even at play, he evidenced no enjoyment. Life was serious business to the capable child. Everything must be perfect to keep him from feeling worried. His teacher began to sense that her prize pupil was in trouble.

■

BARRIERS TO OTHERS

Caroline nearly always received the good citizenship medal. She was invariably considerate of her classmates. It was more important to her to help them win at sports than to be the star player. When she happened into a class with a grouchy teacher, she tried to make the best of it. She was courteous to that teacher, and she influenced her friends to treat the teacher well.

Caroline had an intuitive awareness of others' needs and feelings, and she responded to them with compassion. Even with her parents, she had an unusually positive rapport. She would not tolerate their being too busy and ignoring her needs. In a uniquely loving manner, she would tell them she needed a hug or another specific kind of attention.

Although Caroline did not evidence the severe problems of Beth or Damon, she, too, was at risk. Being too good, even in apparently healthy ways, can cause barriers between the exceptionally good child and her peers. They may feel jealous or inferior; chances are, there will be enough discomfort to estrange them. Goodness of this sort can result in the pain of rejection and loneliness. And there is always the chance that a good child may perceive herself as never quite good enough.

ASSOCIATED SYMPTOMS

Let's return to Beth. She was brought to see a psychiatrist because her goodness was becoming mixed with disturbing symptoms. She had frequent nightmares in which she was struggling to save someone from drowning. The person would not cooperate, and she could feel herself being drawn into cold waves. Just short of giving in to her own death, she would awaken in panic. She had no appetite and even thinking of ice cream could make her feel sick. Nothing was fun with her friends, and she used them as confidantes instead of playmates.

The highest possible degree of goodness in children like Beth may not be enough. It can't make Dad successful; it won't prevent parents' arguments; and it certainly won't make her brother's grades improve. What a predicament for poor Beth! Try as she did, the victim of her nightmares drowned.

At some point, most Beths give up. They have poor self-esteem, and they usually become depressed or even suicidal. And they rarely understand why their best efforts fall short.

Help for Beth, and those like her, lay in understanding that she was responsible only for herself. It was not her task to make her parents happy or her brother a good student. She could clean and straighten up the house;

she could remain caring and helpful to each family member. But she couldn't do their work for them.

■

INVOLVEMENT OF THE WHOLE FAMILY

Answers may be clearly defined, but changes are immensely difficult. The answers for Beth's problems demanded work from the whole family.

Her parents had to realize that Beth's goodness was harmful. They learned that they needed to stop dumping their worries on the dinner table in front of the children. Their arguments and anger—a cover-up for their anxieties—must be expressed outside the range of the children's hearing.

The parents needed to inform their children of any real impending disasters. Children read their parents' faces and know if something is wrong, and they handle truth better than their worst imagined fears. But they do not handle helplessness at all well. So any revelation of adult concerns to kids needs to be accompanied by some plan of action. The children, for example, can understand the need for economizing. They will feel like they're helping by giving up some or even all of their allowances or by not asking for the things they may have demanded. Other job possibilities can give them hope. Saying family prayers and relying on God's power offer great reassurance.

The parents did not recognize the destructive sibling rivalry that was going on. Without realizing the harm it inflicted, they tried to correct their son by asking him to become like his sister. If he would keep his room neat and his study habits up to her standards, things would be fine. But no brother with any self-respect can bear comparisons with a perfect sister! The more the parents tried to make him like her, the more he tried to prove he would be only himself.

At any rate, Beth finally came to grips with the truth—she could not make up to their parents her brother's deficiencies. When she began to allow her imperfections to come out, her brother began to get better. At last, he was not the only "bad guy" around their house.

■ PERFECTIONISM TO THE EXTREME

Damon's family had different dynamics at stake. His parents were perfectionists, too. They worked hard, were honest, and saw only the serious, heavy responsibilities of life as important. Wanting to please them, Damon identified with their habits.

His family did not seek professional help, and Damon had only the help of his teacher. She tried to encourage him to relax. She praised him when he allowed a mistake to slip by his eraser, and she taught him to be more assertive with classmates.

What Damon needed was a change in his home. His parents needed to be less rigid, less compulsive about perfection. Had they laughed more and worried less, their home may well have reflected the warmth Damon needed. His rigidity would quickly have melted in such a climate.

Perfectionistic parents, by the very definition of their

problem, find it difficult to change. They often are unable to admit their perfectionism is a problem. If you are a perfectionist, start thinking in terms of *excellence,* not perfection. Relax and be content to do your best, and help your child follow suit. But be realistic about the best. Usually, this problem is based on fear of the disapproval of others. Try to stop worrying about the judgment of others. If you can please yourself and a loving God, you don't need to please anyone else. As you relax and enjoy life more, you'll find the happiness created to be contagious!

■
SCARED INTO GOODNESS

The behaviors described in Damon may also be caused by abuse. Either verbal or physical abuse can result in a too good child, who is afraid to err in any way. Such goodness is often the heroic effort of a terrified child.

Much as we hate to face the fact, literally millions of children in America are abused annually. Excessive anger and severe punishments leave both emotional and physical scars on young lives. They damage self-esteem and prompt rebellion rather than effect the positive changes parents really seek.

It is obvious that the way to help a child scared into being too good is to stop the abuse. There are many ways to correct and train children; there is no excuse for damaging them by abuse. I know good parents do not want to hurt their children, so if you even suspect you might be abusing your child, contact Parents Anonymous, 520 South Lafayette Park Place, Suite 316, Los Angeles, California 90057.

Parents Anonymous does not promote permissiveness, nor have I ever heard a complaint that the group would discourage biblical, Christian values (though somewhere in this vast country that may have occurred). I have worked with the organization and find it helpful to parents.

■
PLAN AHEAD

Meanwhile, make a plan for use when you know you are becoming irritated with the difficult child in your family. Give your child time to sit and think about whatever wrong he has done. Take that same amount of time to consider these points:

- What is the wrong in this event? Was it deliberate or accidental? (Either needs corrective action.)
- How does this child learn best?
- How can she make amends for the wrong?
- What exact lesson do I want my child to learn from this episode and process?

When you have clear answers to these questions, return to your child, and walk through the corrective action on which you have decided. This plan can prevent the intimidation of a child, making her too good out of fear.

If your too good child is simply superconscientious and sensitive, help is needed to prevent these qualities from becoming out of balance or even compulsive:

- Discuss with your child your observations—that he tries too hard, rarely feels good about himself, and worries.
- Be sure to teach high values regarding healthy goodness while explaining that excessive worry about being too good can destroy one's joy in living.
- Give your child your clear permission to do her best, but discourage the driven quality that concerns you.
- Continue to praise your child for his successes and strivings, but praise him, too, for taking time for having fun and for just "being" instead of always "doing."

Your child may learn to avoid accidents by slowing down. He will make the effort to do so because of your pride and encouragement far more readily than because of his shame or fear. Your child gives up some of his own wishes to follow your rules because he feels your love and concern for him. He wants you to be proud of him.

■

SLIGHTLY OUT-OF-BALANCE GOODNESS

Caroline's goodness was not really harmful. She was a child with an innately pleasant disposition. Her family loved her, and her parents taught well the positive values by which she lived. Her teachers and most of her friends affirmed her with a variety of rewards. And her own sunny nature seemed to feed itself, growing naturally.

Nevertheless, Caroline's goodness created some antagonism from peers who misinterpreted her. They felt she was too good, and jealousy ensued, causing barriers she could not understand.

It was almost a relief to her parents when, on rare occasions, Caroline did misbehave. They discussed such events calmly and helped her make amends. But they were frank about their concerns that her goodness could become not only a barrier but also a burden, too heavy to carry. Every parent should have such a good child!

LOVE CAN MAKE THE DIFFERENCE

If you suspect you have a too good child, take an objective look. Have you been too rigid or strict? Have you, even without realizing it, been abusive? Have you disciplined your child by making statements that resulted in guilt feelings? Have you placed on your child too much responsibility, so she felt unable to keep up with your expectations? Or do you have a child whose goodness is just a little out of balance?

Once you have answered these questions, you can take corrective actions. Unconditional love and acceptance are crucial in every child's emotional development. Only when he occasionally misbehaves, learns how to correct the error, and experiences forgiveness can he truly believe that kind of love. So guide your child in becoming a balanced, whole person who recognizes errors, corrects them, and grows in passing on such unconditional love to others.

11

The Violent Child

Violence is a stark and frightening reality in our world. No longer just a word with its definition portrayed primarily on TV dramas, it is a fact lived out daily. Churches face aggression between children in Sunday school, preschools, and summer camps. School principals find weapons regularly in students' lockers or hidden on their persons. Families suffer violence with increasing frequency, and the media dramatically describe shelters for battered women as becoming a necessary resource for many communities.

Violence, like an ugly, contagious disease, has spread to our teenagers and even children. All too commonly news headlines describe the tragedy of a youngster threatening, harming, or even killing another child. The increase in child, parent, and spouse abuse has become exponential.

Some schools have installed metal detectors through

which all students must pass to enter the building. Uniformed guards and school administrators patrol the halls and peer into rooms trying to locate potential problems and prevent violence. For some twenty years, I have consulted in public schools, and it troubles me greatly to see the development of the need for such strict surveillance.

Examples of juvenile violence could consume this chapter, but perhaps that would waste your time. You read and hear about similar extreme cases of youthful violence in your city regularly.

Instead of such horror stories, let's think about the seeds of violence. Many of the families with whom I work are middle- or upper-income families. Most of them cherish Christian principles and intend to teach them to their children. Yet these are some of the real-life stories of violence that they confront.

■
PERMISSIVENESS

Roger has just turned three. He is exceptionally bright and handsome as a picture. His older sister is a charming, well-mannered kindergartner. When Roger fails to get his way or prefers not to wait his turn, he has several expressive techniques. He may spit on the unfortunate playmate or even bite or kick.

Most preschoolers become angry and lash out physically. The problem with Roger is that no one stops him. There is an endless list of excuses that allow him to act aggressively unchallenged. He's tired. Someone else must have hurt his feelings. He's frustrated by his sister's goodness, and it's sibling rivalry. He may be hungry, or any one of many explanations that allow him to remain obnoxiously uncorrected. How will Roger be likely to behave at age ten or fifteen?

∎
ACTING OUT PAIN IN VIOLENCE

Cheri is a sensitive seven-year-old who has known plenty of tough times. Her parents were serious antagonists, arguing loudly and actually striking each other at times. Finally, they divorced legally, but they remained tied to each other in blame and constant anger. Neither could say a good word about the other but instead heaped condemnation and criticism on the missing spouse. Cheri heard and observed many of their fights.

Her parents were committed Christians who declared their faith in the Bible and their intent to live by its truth. Somehow, this one area of their lives—their marriage relationship—became an exception to their overall beliefs, genuine as they were, and Cheri learned their habits.

When she failed to get the grade she wanted on a test, she threw a tantrum. She blamed her teacher or accused her classroom rival of cheating if she did better. Cheri occasionally went on a rampage through the house, knocking over furniture, breaking dishes or lamps, and kicking holes in the walls.

Currently, I know of at least ten preadolescent children who act as violently as Cheri. They are from godly families who are horrified by their children's actions.

The family members simply feel helpless and do not know how to stop their children. In each case, the entire family is out of control.

■
REBELLIOUS VIOLENCE

Pete is thirteen. His softball uniform and blue cap are immaculate. He has an engaging grin and an open, trusting demeanor. He admits readily that at times he does attack his younger brother, who is his nemesis. It takes very little from the younger boy to send Pete into a rage. You see, he is convinced that his rival has more of the parents' attention and love than he does. This sounds like sibling rivalry, but read on.

Of course, the worse Pete feels, the more he takes out on his brother the anger he has for his parents. Pete has chased his brother with a kitchen knife, but he stated he never intended to cut him. He has grabbed his brother's neck, but he never intended to choke him. Not only does Pete fear that his parents like his brother more, he also believes they expect too much of him. He sees them as rigid, strict, and absolutely unbending in their attitudes. He says he can't do the hard jobs they require, but he fears he can never please them anyway, so why should he try?

Though Pete takes out his rage on his little brother, he feels most angry with his parents. The problem is that he also needs them and even wants to honor them. The only outlet he has found is the vulnerable younger sibling.

Each youngster described here is an example of violence that results from a different base. Roger is the product of a permissive family. His parents believe if they just show him tolerance and patience, he will grow out of his violent behavior and become loving. That outcome is unlikely since he has an intense personality and a high level of energy.

Cheri is one of a large group of children who live in pain-filled families. Her parents' fights and their separation, incomplete due to continued fights, frighten and anger her. She feels no one is there to comfort her. She loves both parents, but each tugs at her loyalties, tearing her heart in two. She is acting out her pain in the violent rage that overwhelms her at times.

Pete is an example of a smaller group of kids, at least in my experience. Their parents are immensely concerned that they become obedient, responsible, and loving. The problem does not lie in the parents' motive of desires for the child, but it rests in their rigid, unbending attitudes. Their heavy controls frustrate a spirited child like Pete who may well take out that anger through violence against others.

■

NEUROLOGICAL CONDITIONS

His cherubic face and mild demeanor deceived me at first. He could not be the difficult child his mother and father described. But when I played with six-year-old Kent, I learned they were right. When I insisted on taking my turn rather than giving every play to him, Kent screamed in rage and sometimes hit me.

When the pieces of a simple puzzle would not fit promptly, he threw them against the wall, kicking and screaming.

The child's story revealed that he had a high fever and convulsions three years ago from a mild case of encephalitis. He was left with mild neurological damage, and as a result, his rage was sometimes uncontrollable.

One study revealed that an inordinately high number of death-row prison inmates had abnormal neurological findings. Someone obtained brain wave tracings (electroencephalograms) on the men and found the majority of them to be abnormal. While this study does not excuse violent crimes, it may help us understand and prevent them.

If your child has a history of illness or an accident that could have left minimal brain damage, take the child for a neurological evaluation. It is especially important if sudden emotional storms that she cannot control overtake your child and she later shows genuine remorse. If your family tree contains relatives with some form of epilepsy, the same recommendation holds.

For violence caused by abnormal neurological conditions, medication is essential. Even if you have strong biases against drugs, overcome them enough to try medical help. The recent discoveries of biochemical factors in brain function are amazing. I believe God has enabled people to unlock the many secrets of human functioning. The massive increase in knowledge has improved the quality of life for many people. Please give your child the benefit of good medical care.

MENTAL ILLNESSES

While you are researching your family tree, look for anyone who may have had manic-depressive or bipolar mental illness. These people live with extreme emotional and psychological highs and then plunge into the trough of despair. We now believe the physical predisposition to this illness is inherited.

Although children rarely, if ever, show the full-blown symptoms of bipolar illness, many of them have the uncontrollable anger that is one evidence of it. It is this uncontrollable anger that erupts in violent behaviors. These kids, like those with neurological damage, are extremely remorseful after their explosions. They, too, can find great improvement with medication. The prescription needs to be supervised by a qualified child psychiatrist or pediatrician. The best option may be to work with your own physician who collaborates with a psychiatrist.

THE ROOTS OF VIOLENCE

Let me take you back to infancy and describe the origin of rage and its expression of violence. Infants are born with only two demonstrable emotions: anger and fear. I was dismayed to learn that, as a pediatrician, I could not elicit or demonstrate any expression of love in a newborn. The helpless dependency of a baby stirs profound loving and protective instincts in healthy parents. But only after some weeks does an infant begin to smile and coo in an expression of pleasure and, eventually, love for another.

An infant demonstrates anger when experiencing pain. When a baby is hungry, feels stomach cramping, or must be pricked to get a blood sample for laboratory tests, for example, a typical reaction takes place. The baby's eyes close tightly, the face grimaces, the hands close into fists, and the arms and legs draw close to the body. Concurrent with the physical actions is a typical cry—the piercing expression of not only pain but the outrage of it all. Parents quickly become familiar with this cry.

Fear elicits a somewhat different response. A baby is born, we know, with the fear of loud sounds and the fear of falling. These inborn fears are life-preserving gifts from God. They prompt a person to avoid fatal falls and to take shelter from possible enemies. The expression of fear can be easily seen by giving a sharp jolt to a baby's crib or by clapping your hands together close to a baby's ear. I don't recommend startling a baby unnecessarily, but as a pediatrician, I had to use those techniques to be certain a newborn could hear and that the nervous system functioned properly.

A child whose nervous system and hearing are normal will react in a typical fashion. The eyes open wide, the arms and legs stretch out instead of flexing inward, and the cry that ensues is characteristically shrill. It sounds quite different from the angry cry.

Attentive parents respond to a child's cry of anger with attention to the pain. They react to the fear with comfort, protection, and reassurance. In either event, the quality and consistency of parents' response to a crying child will create trust and security or, on the other hand, unassuaged anger and insecurity or anxiety.

You will recall that bonding is the process by which an infant becomes attached to parents. It begins at birth and continues at least through the formative years of a child's life. Positive bonding through love, warmth, and responsiveness to the child's needs produces a healthy personality based on trust. Negative bonding can occur through angry, resentful interactions, overpunishment, or abuse. The worst case scenario is the situation in which there is excessive neglect. In this situation there will be partial or total failure of bonding.

When parents respond with all the positive reactions a child needs, the bonds of love and trust grow strong. The secure child learns that crying, or later language, will consistently result in relief of pain and the satisfying sense of having her needs met. Over time, the rage subsides, and the confidence in a positive outcome grows.

A similar dynamic takes place when a child expresses fear. Reassurance, comfort, and physical closeness teach an infant the value of protection. Over time, a child learns to verbalize fears and to cope with them independently.

When parents, however, do not respond in the loving ways just described, an opposite reaction occurs. For example, a parent may feel tired or ill. He may be unable to control his feelings and respond lovingly to a crying child.

If an unhappy parent responds to a child's pain-rage outcry with anger, there are no healing of the pain and no comfort or reassurance for the fears. The infant cannot develop trust in a parent whose anger compounds hers. Either bonding does not occur, or it is negative and takes place about abuse, resulting in a lack of trust. Without trust, there is little security, and only pain and rage are left.

I believe that one fundamental cause of violence is this infantile rage that is either poorly or not at all attended to.

■ Seesawing Emotions

Here is another way of understanding children, anger, and fear. At two, most children are generous with their rebellion, anger, and stretch for independence. Evan was no exception. His mother had to work during the week, but the weekends were their days to play.

One Saturday, his mother had to work overtime, and Evan's grandmother, whom he dearly loved, came to be with him. His mother tenderly told him where she was going, assured him she'd be back, and hugged him. Grandmother happily took over and was busy playing with the blocks on the floor when she realized she was playing alone! Evan had pushed away and was glaring angrily at her.

It was natural that Evan would feel sad over Mommy's absence, so Grandma reached out to hold and comfort the little boy. But he would have none of her aid. He pulled away even farther and continued to scowl. Finally, he arose and stomped angrily away.

Thinking he needed a little time and space to recover, his grandmother waited for his return. When too much time elapsed, however, she went searching for him. She was somewhat surprised to see him staring out the window of his bedroom at the empty driveway below. She was totally unprepared for his angry remarks when he saw her peering in his doorway. "Grandma, you get outta my house!" he shouted.

Anger tends to beget anger, and even the loving grandmother felt herself growing angry. She considered scolding Evan for his rudeness or putting him in time-out. But being a grandmother, she took time to think. She remembered that young children think very simply and concretely. To Evan's childish mind, it seemed if only Grandma were gone, Mommy would be there. And he yearned for his mother.

Instead of venting her anger, Grandma gently interpreted to her hurt and angry grandson what she had just thought out. The magic of her gentle love transformed the angry lad. He admitted the hurt of his loneliness, ran to Grandma's open arms, and allowed her comfort to heal the sense of abandonment he'd felt.

Evan's reaction is an example of any child's seesaw.

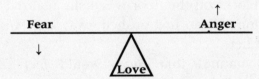

When fear becomes heavy, it will raise the level of anger. Were it not for the presence of love to serve as a balancer, the fear and the anger could become an unending vicious circle.

Fear was Evan's real response to his mother's leaving.

But the fear was unbearable. It raised the level of his anger. Anger feels far more powerful than fear, so the two-year-old intuitively clung to his anger. Had Grandma added her anger to his, you can imagine the powerful bump Evan's fear would have experienced.

The fulcrum of wise love keeps these powerful inborn emotions in balance. When that love is missing, a developing child will face two possibilities: either she will become angrier and that could result in violence, or she will withdraw in excessive fears that may become disabling phobias.

Overprotective love can also have a disabling impact on a child. Without enough freedom to grow and explore his environment, a child may experience two reactions. He may erupt in frustrated rebellion, resisting parental authority. On the other hand, he may withdraw in fear and fail to develop his potential. The rebellion may be expressed in violence, or it may result in sneaking to do the desired thing without the parent's knowledge.

■ Imbalances of Life

These basic concepts can help you understand your child's violence, great or small. Violence can, as described in chapter 5, be verbal as well as physical. In fact, verbal abuse may leave more long-lasting and damaging scars than physical mistreatment. Screaming, name-calling, and severely critical tirades leave deep injuries in the soul of their victim.

■ Treating Permissiveness

Sometimes violence emerges out of permissive parenting as you read about earlier with Roger. In adolescence, the fruit of childhood permissiveness ripens. Teens intuitively know they need boundaries. Again and again such kids test their parents. *Maybe this time she'll have the courage to tell me no,* they think. And each time the edict fails to be given, the kids are disappointed.

One teenage girl told me her story with this theme. Throughout her childhood, her mother rarely restricted her. Insightful beyond her years, Angie told me she had come to believe her mother did not love her. In more and more daring ways, she tested authority—her mother, her teachers and, finally, the law. Always she yearned for a strong voice to declare, "No, Angie! I care about you. I won't let you do these risky things!"

That voice was not heard until she stood before the judge of a juvenile court. Angie had stolen a car, driven it illegally, and wrecked it. The judge finally made the statement that Angie longed to hear. And Angie's mother wept over her "wayward" child's actions. Then, Angie told me, for the first time in her young years, she began to believe her mother cared.

Violence, with its immeasurable pain and rage, all too often is rooted in permissive parenting. Parent, you must understand that your child's defiance and apparent rebellion are instinctive ways of testing how much you care. There are three questions every child deserves to have answered:

1. Do you care about me enough to make me obey?
2. Are you wise enough to find a way to establish boundaries for me?
3. Are you strong enough to follow through so I can lean on you in my weakness?

If you fail in these three testing areas, you and your child will pay a heavy price.

Permissive parenting is difficult to correct, but it can be done:

1. Make a definite decision to set clear boundaries.
2. Discuss them with your child, explain the reasons for them, and seek her ideas in establishing them.
3. Set up fair and meaningful consequences for failure to stay within the boundaries and rules.
4. Follow through kindly but firmly and with great consistency.
5. It will be the parents who will carry the primary responsibility for these changes, so stick with these steps!

■ Treating Violence in an Acting Out Child

Remember Cheri? She was behaving violently around her house during the aftermath of her parents' divorce. In families that live in pain, much help is needed, not only for the child but also for the entire system. Here are helps for healing and stopping the violence as well:

1. Get help for the hurts. Start with the person who hurts the most. In Cheri's case that probably was her father. But Mom was hurting, too. As the par-

ents become stronger, the child will feel secure and less angry, so her violence will decrease.

2. Develop a support system of friends and relatives who can help the entire family. Listening, offering explanations to children, and helping each family member see both the needs and the feelings of the others will facilitate family healing.

3. Helping to locate and use community resources is often beneficial for hurting families. Financial, legal, counseling, and medical resources can seem impossible to locate when one is undergoing great stress. A friend may be immensely helpful in this way.

At times it's quite a challenge to get a violently acting out child to explain her pain. Someone outside the family or often a professional counselor is needed to discover and treat the exact cause of a child's pain. It's well worth the effort to find and use such resources.

∎ Treating the Violence of a Rebellious Child

I had seen Pete's parents several times before he was finally able to visit me. By then I knew about their excessively rigid way of dealing with their children, but I also knew how much they loved them. Helping them and Pete became a fairly easy task:

1. They began to see Pete's point of view, and in a safe place, he could admit that much of his angry violence was taken out on his brother instead of being expressed to them.

2. They understood that they had to make the family

rules, specifically those that pressured Pete, more flexible. Yet they knew he needed consistency.

3. They discovered that Pete had difficulty feeling their love when they chronically displayed disapproval and anger toward him.

For rebellious violence, the antidote is gentler and more flexible parenting. Teaching a child how to verbalize his angry feelings instead of expressing them through violence is also crucial. Many children also need some safe physical action to give vent to the anger—hitting a mattress or a punching bag will metabolize those chemicals the body puts out under stress. We call these chemicals stress hormones, and there are more than twenty of them that the body manufactures. Exercise burns them up, helping a person finish off a given episode of stress.

■

PREVENTING VIOLENCE

Preventing violence takes a loving heart, a little of God's great wisdom, and a lot of commitment, even when it's not convenient. Here are some common-sense guidelines to help you achieve a positive attitude that will facilitate your task:

- Understand your child's needs by observing and asking about needs and feelings. Teach her how to verbalize them, and respond to her words with care, protection, guidance, or whatever the need demands.
- Believe this truth: no one else can love your child quite like you, the parent, can. Your child must *feel*

your love. He needs to hear your expression of caring in word and deed regularly.

- Let love motivate you to endure the inconveniences that good training and discipline demand. Many parents fall into habits of permissiveness because they become weary and just give up. Hanging in there is necessary to provide the essential ingredient of consistency.

- Use your love to help you build a strong, healthy marriage because it takes at least two to do the job. If you are a single parent, find relatives or friends to back you up and provide the support you need. Groups of single parents can be of great help to each other.

- Settle for a little less material success in the interest of greater success in child rearing. Many parents become overly focused on material security and unwittingly sacrifice the time and their presence with the child.

- Take the trouble to control your anger, overcome your lassitude, and learn the best ways to balance your parenting. Your negative behaviors not only hurt your child but also become a role model for her to follow.

- Be to your child what you will long for him to be to you when you are older.

TEACH YOUR CHILD PROTECTION

From current statistics, it seems apparent that the effective prevention of violence in our communities is a long way off. Meanwhile your child may need to know self-defense today. Many parents have taught their children never to fight. Only today a mother asked me, "How do I help a child who has been taught not to hurt others but who is being hurt physically and verbally by other children?"

I am sad to say the time has come for many families to reconsider this extremely pacifist stand. The basic values of turning the other cheek and giving the coat when the cloak has been stolen still must be taught. They are valid, self-protective concepts. But when others are allowed, unchecked, to become ever more belligerent bullies, a champion may be needed.

A favorite hero of mine is David, the Old Testament shepherd boy who became a king. As a lad, he killed the bully Goliath who had intimidated the entire Israeli army. God honored him. Now let me hasten to say, it is not okay for your child to kill a bully! But the biblical message I suggest is that enough is enough!

So teach your child some self-protective techniques. Classes in many cities teach a number of precautions and modes of self-protection. As soon as your child is old enough, send him to a class. It may well be in your interest to attend, too.

Teach your child to run. And help your child know it may not be cowardly to run, though some of her peers will accuse her of cowardice. Advise her on where to run and how to call for help. At school, for example, it is usually wise to seek the help of staff persons. The administrators need to know when violence is happening or being threatened.

Obviously, bullies will threaten to get even with a student who tells on them. And they often follow through with threats. You may encourage your child to tell you the problem and let you find a way to report it. Sticky situations need great caution in handling due to the power of student gangs.

In my city and many others, it is not uncommon for children to be hurt by other kids while walking to school or waiting at a bus stop. Even abduction and murder occur. Though these events may happen in any neighborhood, they are more frequent where violence is more common.

In your community, you may need to accompany your child to school. And you may decide to move or to find a private school to ensure your child's safety.

Common sense and caution are still effective enough in most areas. The importance of parental protection and guidance must be balanced with confidence in each child's ability to learn and practice precautions.

■

VIOLENCE OR LOVE?

To summarize, preventing violence demands good parenting skills and role modeling. Develop clearly defined policies by which your family lives. Teach and enforce them by establishing consequences for misbehaving and using natural consequences of poor decisions. Always express pride in your child's efforts to do well and encourage ongoing growth and improvement.

Treating a violent child requires time and energy. Using the suggestions offered will help most children learn compliance. In cases where nothing seems to work, professional help should be found. An accurate diagnosis and guidance along with carefully prescribed medication can transform most situations.

I must add that in the case of neurologically impaired children, or those whose violence has reached a stage where safety and even lives are at risk, hospitalization may be required. Even a few weeks of observation, twenty-four-hour structure, medication, and family therapy and guidance can work the beginnings of miracles.

You can solve the problem of violence in your difficult child and your home. When enough families work this solution, our communities will become safe, and the quality of life we all desire can become a reality.

12

Indifference

The classroom was strangely still. Most of the students were at lunch. Only Lowell and I remained behind: he, because his teacher was at her wit's end, and I, because I hoped to help her win Lowell's cooperation. Lowell had a respectable IQ, not gifted, but high average. No known tests had revealed any type of learning disability. He did not register on the scales testing attention deficit disorder, and yet he was failing almost every subject.

Over the decades, I had worked with children suffering from most of the catalogued maladies. Usually, kids sensed my caring nature and in time would respond to my overtures. But not Lowell! I tried humor, seriousness, and a touch of firmness with no success—not even a little bit!

When I told him an anecdote showing I could understand kids, he looked through me as if I were transparent. When I asked a question, he often refused to answer at all, his well-masked face directed toward the floor. But most annoying of all was Lowell's occasional response to a question. His slender shoulders would rise and then mutely fall in a gesture that clearly shrugged me off his back. From his tightly clenched jaws a somewhat guttural sound would push its way out. By stretching my imagination, I could interpret that sound to mean, "I don't know!"

Lowell did know very well, but he had learned to cope with invasive people. He neither liked nor trusted grown-ups, especially women! That much was quite evident. What Lowell did not know was that I had once behaved exactly as he was doing. I understood his techniques and their origin.

He had endured so many lectures and so much nagging that his only defense lay in pretending not to hear. He acted as if he really did not know and, even worse, he no longer cared. And I understood that any child can take only so much of an adult's repeated disapproval without indifference setting in. Lowell was definitely indifferent.

When I told him I suspected that both his mom and his teacher were "on his back" a lot, he looked at me with amazement. Had I been reading his mind, or had I listened in on his last evening at home? Of course, I'd done neither, but I'd lived through all sides of his unhappy situation.

"I DON'T KNOW"

When I was a child, I strove with all my might for the perfection required to please my mother. She set high standards for living, and in one area especially, she was meticulous. The house must be sparkling clean at least once a week. Our entire week was ordered around routine household chores. Washing was always done on Monday, ironing and mending on Tuesday, gardening or lawn work on Wednesday and Thursday. Friday was flexible but busy. Saturday was reserved for thorough housecleaning. I awoke week after week vowing and praying that I could this day do my assigned task perfectly. It was my job to dust. I started upstairs shaking out the lovely embroidered dresser scarves mother's hands had artfully designed. I dusted in every crevice I could find and then moved on to the next rooms. I inspected my work and felt it was perfect. *Today, Mom will be proud of my work,* I thought. But that didn't happen.

As a child, I began to suspect that some evil genie blinded my eyes because Mother could always find some small area I'd missed. And then I was in for a lecture, usually a fairly lengthy one holding out no hope that I could ever do it right. I gave up caring. I was going to hear those critical words anyway, so why should I try? I was allowed no defense and no comeback. Even when she asked me a question, I learned Lowell's response: a shrug of my shoulders and a muttered "I don't know" would result in her eventual silence.

As an adult, I recognize that my sullen indifference

must have hurt and frustrated my mother. And I now understand that she felt she was neglecting the necessary training if she approved too quickly of my efforts. I know that she believed if I were less than perfect, it was ultimate judgment that I must face. So I have gladly forgiven that demanding taskmistress. But I have not lost the traces of scars that too much disapproval carved into my spirit.

REPEATED LECTURES

Although I ceremoniously vowed that I would never scold my children like my mother scolded me, I'm sorry to say, I broke that vow. I was blessed with three delightful children—the greatest joys of my life— until my grandchildren were born! The middle child, my only son, was a special delight as a toddler. He was exuberant in his welcome homes and full of vitality, sensitive and always kind.

He was also a daydreamer. He was so intensely involved in his play and creations that he forgot the rest of the world. He'd promise to come to dinner "in a minute," but he'd fail to show up for fifteen. He'd be glad to feed the dog "pretty soon," but the dog might go to bed hungry.

Knowing I had to teach him to be responsible, I would remind him of his tasks. And yet again and again I would remind him with rising intensity in my heart and my voice. To my chagrin, I could hear the echoes of my mother's disapproving lectures. Even more to my dismay, I saw mirrored the shrugging shoulders and heard the muttered "I don't know" of my childhood. What was I doing to my dearly loved son?

∎
A HAPPY-GO-LUCKY AIR

Jill showed a perpetual smile, at times somewhat cynical, whenever I saw her. Her parents' faces by contrast were rarely free of a scowl or a look of worry. They had calls from Jill's teachers at least weekly. At age eleven, she was full of spirit, wanted to laugh, and hated to study.

At home, Jill took certain perverse delight in tormenting her brother. She conveniently forgot to do her chores and often spoke rudely to her mother.

They had, I was told by Jill's parents, tried everything to correct her attitude and behavior. "But nothing," they said mournfully, "seems to get to her. She just doesn't care!" They had tried depriving her of privileges to watch TV, ride her bike, or be with friends; they even grounded her alone in her room. Indeed, Jill allowed no consequence to touch her. She had learned that if she made herself indifferent, she did not suffer remorse, and her parents gave up. She could get back her privileges, continue her happy-go-lucky lifestyle, and basically take control of her young world. The problem was that her control was putting her on well-lubricated skids to failure and serious trouble.

THE EXPLANATION

In one of these examples, you may see traces of yourself and your child. So let's uncover how such indifference develops, not just in the case of Jill, but almost any child:

- There is always an area of concern and disagreement between parent and child. Lowell's mother and teacher wanted him to succeed in school, but he had other important areas of focus, namely, fun!
- The adults nudged and reminded the children of their duties without results. They lectured and meted out consequences to no avail.
- Resentments, disapproval, and ill will grew in both parents and children. I know my mother was terribly frustrated with my work and my attitude. I certainly reciprocated.
- Instead of changing methods, the parents (including me!) tried harder—repeating mistakes even more intensely.
- The ultimate problem became one of deeply ingrained hurt, too severe to bear, so each child learned how not to care and became indifferent.

THE SOLUTIONS

Perhaps using myself as an example can reassure all of you parents of indifferent kids. If I could find some answers that worked, so can you! You may use my solutions or create your own. Just recognize that there are answers.

∎ Face It

For me, the first step to a solution was facing the issue. I wanted more than anything to be a good mother. It took a monumental shock to awaken me to the reality that I, more than my son, was at fault. Be aware that you, the parent, may need to be the starting point for change.

∎ Decide to Change

Let your awareness of your faults motivate you to decide to change. How often people say, "I need to change," or "I'll really try," but they don't reach the point of decisive commitment. Real decisions say, "I will, and here's how I will."

∎ Develop a Definite Plan

It helps to write this out. When I realized I was making my son's life and mine miserable, I found a time to talk through with him how we would change my faulty parenting.

∎ Follow Through

The best plan is useless unless you follow through. Find some help—a friend, your spouse, and best of all your child—and seek their encouragement, reminders, and support.

■ **Persist**

Often parents give up just when they almost had it made. Hanging in there is a cliche with meaning.

APPROACHES THAT WORK

■ **Doing It on His Own**

It was no easy job to help Lowell's mom and his current teacher see their role in his behaviors. They firmly stood by their beliefs that their task was to make Lowell do his work and they would continue reminding (nagging) him until he did it. Never mind that the technique hadn't worked over five past teachers and school years; they were together in it. Nearly at the end of elementary school, however, a special teacher and his mom decided to try a new approach.

Lowell's mom and teacher agreed that passing the fifth grade would be up to him. They admitted their efforts were only making everyone miserable. The teacher explained exactly what he would have to do to pass. His mother discussed some ideas about quiet study time in the evening, but she assured him she would not nag him.

Lowell, you can imagine, was profoundly perplexed. It was a whole new way of life, and he was unfamiliar with the new turn. At first he reveled in the indescribably good feeling of freedom. No one was on his back. He felt floaty light. His papers, however, kept coming back marked *F* or *Incomplete.* He waited for the familiar scowls and lectures, but he found only friendly looks and no comments.

After several days, Lowell decided they meant business. He found the paper with his assignments carefully written out. He didn't even wait for his mother's structured study time. Pushing his sister out of the way, he turned off the TV and began to work. By the end of the year, Lowell had completed his assigned work and passed—barely. The significant point was that he'd done it on his own!

When you are reasonably certain your child can do assigned tasks, your best approach may well be that of Lowell's mother. Let him do it on his own. The natural consequences of possible failure may be his best discipline.

In some cases, really tough kids would let themselves fail, believing at the last minute someone would rescue them. It's extremely important not to rescue a passive, indifferent child; the child must feel the pangs of pain her poor choices create. A lost year in school, planned carefully, is a small price to pay for learning to exchange indifference for caring and passive resistance for successful achievement.

■ Alternating Criticism with Praise

My childhood could have improved immensely had my mother known how much I craved her approval. Had she at least alternated weeks, praising me one week and correcting the next, I could have borne her criticism. But when, in my memory at least, her approval was never won, I had to quit trying and become uncaring to survive psychologically. I feel most fortunate that through some of my training, I reached the point of understanding and forgiving her.

■ Learning from Consequences

I'm grateful that I reached the point of my emotional healing in time to save my son from some of the ongoing pain I was inflicting. Like those of my mother, my intentions were fine, but my methods were absolutely terrible. After ten years of nagging and sometimes cruel scoldings, I carefully planned a talk with him.

Painfully realizing how I had hurt him, I began with a heartfelt apology. I confessed that I had focused so completely on a few areas of weakness that I had not commented on his strengths. As I began to list them, I nearly wept out of the sadness of my revelation. My son was full of generosity, sensitivity, caring, and compassion. And I had lectured him for being unaware of time limits and forgetful about duties! In the amazing grace of children, my son freely forgave me. Together, we worked a plan for his being responsible for his duties. You see, I had been the responsible one—unknowingly robbing him of the needed lessons in learning from natural consequences.

I often bit my tongue and he frequently forgot some chores, but over time we made the change. When he forgot to get up and missed the school bus, he walked to school. That happened only once, and I managed to refrain from saying, "I told you so!" When he forgot to feed the dog, he did not get to eat until it was done. Bit by bit, we found the results of his irresponsibility, and he learned through them instead of my lectures.

∎
BEYOND POWER STRUGGLES

J ill represents another angle of indifference. She is not just passively resistant but actively manipulative. Probably by accident at first, she learned that her parents would give in if she didn't respond to their consequences. No doubt she was also a strong-willed child who intuitively held out to have her way.

What I have observed about kids like Jill lies below their surface masks of indifference. These children, like most, care all too much about their parents' approval. They want it. But they also want their own way. Unlike the conscious deceit of the manipulative child, they stumble on to the fact that they can get their way passively with only moderate parental disapproval. They pick up on the idea that their parents are a bit proud of their cleverness. Disliking their sense of weakness, they struggle quietly for power and misperceive their ability to get their way as power. On the one hand, they enjoy their power, but on the other hand, they experience twinges of guilt over taking unfair advantage. Over time their consciences become calloused, depriving them of the blessing of real guilt, and those callouses add to their facade of indifference.

Parents of children like Jill need a different solution from those suggested earlier. They first must make sure they understand the power struggle and guilt complex. Then they must find their own real strength. Because of experience and age, parents are always wiser than the brightest child.

As Jill's parents became more confident, they were less frequently deceived by her. Instead of giving in to her unwise power, they retained control. They explained to Jill some of the unhealthy interactions that had grown among them. They asked her to let go of some of her apparent power and to allow a warm friendship to replace it. They began to share fun activities with her as well as require some responsibilities from her.

Jill finally discussed with her parents their goals for her life—not really too different from her own. And all three of them searched for consequences that would help her learn how to attain those goals.

Through openness, love, and logic, the family corrected problems even the severest punishments had missed. Basic understanding, creative thinking, teamwork, and persistence can solve almost every problem.

Children's indifference is usually directly proportional to adults' overinvolvement and nagging. The more parents make the child's problems theirs, the more likely they are to assume the responsibility for solving them. Answers lie, then, in focusing the child on her own problems and helping her find the right answers. Certainly, parents and teachers need to show their interest in both the child and her problems, but this must be balanced with a staunch refusal to coerce the child, establishing no-win power struggles. Patiently wait for the child to assume her own responsibility.

Confidence in your own good parenting and in your child's ultimate abilities to make it will help you through the struggle with your indifferent child.

13
Self-Pity

When Ruth was just a child, she suffered from repeated strep infections. Believe it or not, there was a time before penicillin or any antibiotics. Some recovered from infections, others were left with disabling conditions, and still others died. In that era, Ruth became ill repeatedly. The infections were bad enough, but their complicating aftermath became life threatening.

Ruth was a member of a large and very busy family, so day-to-day attentions were necessarily limited. But when she was ill with high fevers and a throat so painfully swollen she could hardly swallow, her busy parents somehow found the time for her. Her mother brought her special soft foods on a tray, and her hardworking father read to her in the evening until his eyes fell shut in spite of his efforts to stay awake. Being sick was no fun, but it did have its fringe benefits.

During her school years, Ruth discovered that her

family rallied about persons with any and all kinds of problems. When her sister became anorexic, everyone tried to think of something special to nourish her. When her brother experienced a series of nosebleeds, even the doctor was called—a big event in those days. When her schoolteacher was unpleasant, the family cared and gave both sympathy and encouragement.

Families who were friends of Ruth's parents often came to visit. While the children played, Ruth would creep near the parlor where special guests were entertained. She could hear her mother's tender voice trying to comfort one in tears. Her father's husky voice chimed in with his wise counsel. Early on, Ruth learned that pain of both body and heart was worthy of attention. Furthermore, she came to recognize that compassion and tender care were the best healers.

All of those influences left a positive mark on Ruth's developing personhood. But there was a trace of a harmful element mixed in. Ruth did not understand that she could get attention for being healthy and functioning independently. She believed it took her pain for her busy family to find the time for her.

Unknowingly, the girl looked for problems, and by magnifying them just a bit, she could gain all sorts of attention from many people. She gladly gave equal time and concern to others. But it was primarily through problems that she related to people.

Ruth eventually understood the game she had been playing. She learned that people soon tired of the game and began to avoid her. She also discovered that she could solve most of her problems, and she began to do that. Furthermore, she found that she had many delightful ideas, interests, and activities to share that brought her more friends and attention than she could have imagined.

■

COMFORT AND CATASTROPHES

What a delightful baby Darla was! She was born with a gentle personality; she slept through the night from only a few days of age. She learned quickly, loved everyone, and was compliant to a fault. If she ever did suffer pain, she cuddled up until she felt better. It was easy and satisfying to her mother to comfort her.

Darla's mother was somewhat akin to Ruth. She saw in her child something of her own past wherein she had experienced love through pain and its comfort. At any rate, she became a first-class comforter. And Darla seemed to thrive on it—for a time.

The time came, however, when Darla's needs for comfort grew at an alarming rate. Nearly every day a near or real catastrophe had to be related. Her teacher was expecting too much, and this year she could not keep up. Yes, she had done well last year, but perhaps this year she had "maxed" out and would fail and be disgraced. Her best friend had been mean and had ignored her. Her father did not have time for her. Always, there was trouble.

Darla's mother checked with some of her teachers. Their report was of a happy, energetic, and all-round good student. Reassured on the one hand, Mother became concerned on the other. Perhaps she had enjoyed comforting her child too much. Could she have trained her daughter to bond with her primarily through problems? As she took an objective overview of her parenting, she decided that was exactly what she had done.

Slowly and quietly, Darla's mom began to change her approach. Whenever possible, she would greet her daughter after school with a funny story from her own day. If Darla began to present a problem, Mom would listen, ask questions, and guide Darla to her own solutions.

Mom began to feel they were on a much healthier basis until one day Darla came in after school dramatically stricken with grief. She threw herself on the sofa and sobbed out her woes. After a bit of studied neglect, her mother sat down beside her and silently stroked her disheveled hair. Gradually, the sobs subsided. Darla opened her tearful eyes wide and asked, "Mom, you know I think I kind of like feeling bad! And that's not good, is it?"

What a rare event it is for an adolescent to stumble on to the causes of her problem! Together, she and her mom worked out some solutions.

■

DEMANDS FOR ATTENTION

Excessive self-pity emerges almost always from a situation similar to Ruth's or Darla's. From circumstances that just happened, Ruth discovered how to get extra attention. It felt good to have someone care about her, and she could not trust anyone to unconditionally accept her. Unconsciously, her lifelong habits silently taught her people cared most when she hurt.

Darla was rarely ill, yet she did, by an accident of her personality and her mom's, find out that her most intensely bonding events occurred around emotional pain.

When others no longer respond to frequent demands for sympathy, children prone to self-pity will resort to giving it to themselves. They withdraw from those who love them the most and essentially lick their wounds in private. They can develop a spirit of bitterness and resentment that further estranges them from others and blocks out the healing of love.

Usually, such children along with their parents need professional counseling. Parents can learn how to give positive attention. Children can learn to ask clearly and specifically for attention in ways that are satisfying and positive rather than destructively pitying.

Darla learned that solution after her discovery of her paradoxical enjoyment of bad feelings. She would often go to her parents and ask for hugs or remind them that they hadn't talked much for a while. And they were most willing to respond.

■

WHINING

In young children, self-pity is often expressed in whining, babyish behaviors. Many parents have come to me extremely irritated over a child's whining.

Most parents gruffly tell the child, "Grow up and quit being such a baby!" While one can empathize with the frustration of the parents, their irritation can only make the problem worse.

Whining children, too young to understand and verbalize their needs and feelings, are pleading to have more babying. They need exactly that. To prevent the whining from becoming worse and ending up in excessive self-pity, you must do *three* things:

1. Soothe the immediate episode of whining with a calm, firm voice. Saying, "Sit in time-out with your bear," instead of requiring the child to sit alone feeling even worse, is a great plan.
2. Plan scheduled times to give some cuddling attention to a whining child. There may even be times that holding will help during the whining. Some people believe that giving attention during a "whining attack" could reinforce it. Just be sure to give plenty of warm, nurturing attention at many times if you are one of those folks.
3. Convey to a whining child that you can understand he needs to be little at times. (This pattern often develops after the birth of a new baby or in the wake of another big change.) Tell the child to come to you and ask for a cuddle instead of whining. If the child can't talk yet, you, the parent, must watch for the signs of sadness or feelings of neglect. Offer your love and presence before the whining starts.

It may take courage to try this method of handling. But try to trust me! The rewards will surprise you. And you will see that saturating a child's attentional needs will strengthen her foundation of trust and bonding. After a time, the child will climb off your lap and move on to more independent behaviors. If you're like me, you'll feel pretty nostalgic for more cuddling yourself!

Whatever the expression of self-pity, it becomes a practice that is difficult to live with. Understand that it is a habit, learned inadvertently from life experiences. It temporarily feels good and usually solicits sympathy from others, which feels even better! By recognizing the need that underlies this feeling, you can relieve or even solve the problem. Provide adequate attention, lots of love, and plenty of laughter and fun for your self-pitying child. He'll soon trade the old habits for the new sense of happiness.

Sex

14

In recent months, at least half a dozen parents have approached me about sexual issues affecting their children. None of the children was a teenager. The oldest was seven. At that tender age and younger, the children had either heard about adult sexual acts or had tried performing them.

Today I learned from two sources, one a physician, that in an East Coast city, condoms were being given to boys as young as fifth graders by the school staff. In their schools over 30 percent of sixth-grade boys were sexually active, and 17 percent of fifth-grade boys were. The school staff felt the urgent need to protect the children from causing pregnancies among their child partners and to protect them from sexually transmitted diseases (STD's).

Apparently few, if any, voices are being raised to say to children, "No, you may not have sex. I will protect you from becoming exposed to deadly diseases. I am your parent. I will not let you grow up too soon. Sex is for marriage, and you are too young for that!" Parents have abdicated their responsibility, and children are paying the price.

The sexual relationship is a beautiful symbol of spiritual intimacy. It is a demonstration of God's provision for companionship between the first human beings. It is the means through which marital fidelity and intimacy are expressed. Its most sacred purpose is the loving conception of a new human being, created again in the image of God, as were Adam and Eve in the dawn of creation.

How indescribably sad that sex has degenerated to so much less. For too many people, teens and adults, sex has become an exploit of one person against another, an act about which to brag to peers. It has become to some an expression of rebellion. One young woman said that at thirteen she would sneak out of her house and sleep with boys in her neighborhood: "If my dad could have an affair [and she knew he had], it had to be okay for me to have sex." Not only was she rebelling against her father's rules for her, but she was following his poor example.

Sex has become a form of recreation for teenagers in school hideaways, a pastime during time-out at school sports events, and something to do until parents get home from work. Adults use sex for equally shallow reasons. It's a sport to be engaged in during the lunch hour, on the way home from work, or at the whim of the people involved.

There are a number of reasons why kids become sexually active. One is that it is exciting; it feels good. "If it feels good, do it!" said a once popular bumper sticker. There's no doubt, for most people, having sex feels good. If it happens to result in an infection, medical science can usually fix that. If it results in an unwanted pregnancy, current laws allow medical technology to take care of that. Many young people learn that sexual activity can and often does result in heartbreak. When the search for pleasure results in broken relationships as she seeks new and different partners, it becomes exploitive and selfish. It then is not making love but creating pain.

And what of the moral issues involved? When wedding vows lose their validity for parents, what are children to think about honesty? How can they be held to any commitment when their role models do not show them how? Children are keenly aware of their parents' beliefs and practices. When parents say one thing and do another, children become confused. And many parents admittedly feel so guilty, they let down their rules and allow total freedom to their children.

On a late night television talk show, a father and two sons and a mother and a daughter were interviewed regarding the rules about sexual behaviors. The mother had at least tried to establish some boundaries. But when her early adolescent child slept with the mother's boyfriend, it was too much for her. She stated that she gave up and allowed her daughter to do as she wished. The very young teen boys had never had sexual restrictions set by their father. The three of them brashly stated for uncounted viewers to hear that any and all sex was allowed, no holds barred.

Perhaps the show picked up some extreme cases with which to shock viewers. But the statements were made, and many a youngster almost certainly decided that night, "If they can do it, so can I." While TV may at times portray American life and values (or the lack thereof), it assuredly also influences them.

■
SEXUAL ACTING OUT

Engaging in sexual intimacy prematurely results in the risk or reality of serious diseases and nearly always the grievous loss of sound moral values and self-respect. Such sexual behavior commonly exploits others and ends in disillusionment. Yet having sex is so exciting and the instinctive urge is so powerful, it may become an addiction. As time goes on, more energy is spent with a less-exciting return until the person becomes jaded and disappointed. When new partners and exotic methods fail to produce the sought-after excitement, depression may well result.

Sexual acting out is often a means of proving one's sexiness. And to all too many young people, being sexy is a measure of personal value. Unless they are sought after by many persons of the opposite sex, they feel something is dreadfully wrong with them. Their personal values are confused.

LONGING FOR INTIMACY

In my opinion, there is a silent, deep reason for sexual promiscuity among young people. I suspect it is true for many adults as well. That reason lies in the search for intimacy.

Because of the mobility of nuclear families, relatively few children grow up near their grandparents or other relatives. Entire families grieve over the repeated loss of loved ones due to frequent moves demanded by jobs. Grieving parents have limited energy for lavishing love on their children.

The growth in divorce rates has created even greater loss with even deeper grief. Grieving single parents can rarely provide the protection and supervision children need. Many struggling single moms I know call their children after school to be sure they are safe at home. And many of those children I know plan exactly when to leave after that call or whom to invite over till Mom gets home.

With the inborn human yearning for touch and closeness, the temptation to engage in the ultimate physical intimacy seems too great to resist. As our society becomes increasingly selfish and guarded against trusting and being let down, we can hardly expect any other development. The cultural trends place on each of us who retains positive values about wholesome love the need to share and teach these precepts. We must begin with our families and extend this teaching to everyone who will listen. We can make a difference!

PEER PRESSURE

Peer pressure is another major factor in sexual promiscuity. One committed mother I know well chose to work in school so she could be with her children and provide the essential supervision. She had explicitly taught good values and raised her family within the circle of their church's help. She was shocked to arrive home one afternoon to discover her daughter of fourteen years and the girl's boyfriend undressing in her bedroom.

Fortunately, the daughter was sincerely repentant, and as mother and child wept together, she explained, "I'm the only one in my whole group who hasn't had sex. They think I'm a prude and they laugh at me. Mom, I can't take it anymore!" She had talked her boyfriend into helping her out of her status problem. My friend was able to help her daughter reverse the situation. Her daughter learned to be proud of her values, and she stopped caring what her group members said.

INFLUENCE OF MEDIA

In my local grocery store is a large display of magazines. We have a wonderful manager who seems to make some effort to hide the pornographic ones from young eyes. But countless stores lack a conscientious manager. They know that sex sells, and they promote the most sexually scintillating stuff.

It is tempting to blame pornography for the sexual activity of young people. But the blame lies elsewhere— in the hearts of parents and other adults who starve their children of love, fail to provide protection, and allow their lives to be bare of wholesome influences. Children are curious about sex, but when given a choice, most of them would rather ride a Ferris wheel or roller coaster or play backyard baseball with other kids than focus on pornographic magazines.

The negative influences of pornography exert their greatest impact on the most vulnerable children. Those who have been exposed to explicit sexual information by the adults in their lives develop a fascination with it. On the other extreme, children who have been overprotected, who have not had adequate teaching about sexual matters by their parents, are likely to have great curiosity. Pornography is not likely to appeal to children who have plenty of parental love, wholesome, creative activities, and adequate, appropriate information carefully taught by their parents.

Please do not misunderstand me. I am against pornography, especially for vulnerable kids! But blaming it for the sexual problems of children in some degree allows parents to abdicate *their* responsibility. Teach your children about their sexuality, their sexual responsibilities, and help them acquire healthy, wholesome sexual attitudes.

Another influence from the media concerns me, and that is the presence of cable TV in children's bedrooms. Even parents who carefully supervise the programs kids watch in their living rooms seem incredibly oblivious to the scenes their children watch after going to bed. Kids with remote controls are slick at fooling parents who come around now and then to check.

One elementary school lad of twelve, preoccupied with sexual talk and drawings, told me of another source of sexual input. His parents rented extremely explicit movies and then acted them out in their living room. The child happened on their routine one night and became hooked. He listened and observed, finding he could peek at them and never be caught.

Yet one more caution. A boy of eight had been ostracized in his neighborhood after sex play with several children. His bewildered parents could not imagine where he had been initiated into knowledge of those activities.

In the course of answering routine questions he related that he and his parents, on a recent vacation, had stayed in a lovely hotel. While his parents were out for a brief errand, he had flipped the controls looking for some favorite cartoons. To his utter amazement, he switched to a station showing an extensive preview of so-called adult shows. The sights had so intrigued and stimulated him, he could not block them from his memory. Later he had tried to act them out. It took months to relieve the guilt and preoccupation with adult sexual acts those few moments had caused.

Parent, you can hardly be too careful. Guard your child against a precocious sexual awakening. If that has already happened, encourage her to talk about it with you. Explain calmly to her that sexual intimacy is a beautiful experience for married people that she can anticipate when she gets married. Then help her file away those sexual thoughts and pictures, pouring her youthful energies into wholesome activities suitable for kids. There is no substitute for a parent's presence in protecting a child from inappropriate TV shows or movies. No child needs a TV in her room unless she has a mobility impairment. You'll also guard against spoiling your child with too many things, such as a TV in her room!

■
CARING MATTERS

Some years ago a dear friend came to my office with her daughter, who was in her late teens. The mother learned that the young woman had been sexually involved with a young man. The daughter seemed amazed that her mother should care because "everybody else" was doing it. What was more, she adamantly stated that she had no intentions of stopping. I did my best to reason with her. It seemed apparent the young man had no real commitment to her. She was going along with his wishes partly because she was afraid of losing him. Trying to help her see that he might be using her seemed futile. After a long hour, the two left me feeling defeated.

It was several weeks before they returned, and I was amazed at the changes in the faces of both of them. With almost a sound of elation, the daughter told me she had decided to break off her relationship with the boyfriend. The mother's face beamed as the daughter chattered on. Later I asked the mother what she had done to effect the miraculous change. She said she had prayed a lot, and she had not allowed herself to believe her child's behavior was okay. In a quietly powerful manner, she had willed the change to take place.

I'm not naive enough to believe these steps will work for every parent. You may have "willed" such changes for your child without results. On the other hand, I see many more parents who do give in to their child's rebelliousness and tacitly seem to consent. Find a balance between nagging and hopeless power struggles and passively giving up. Sometimes influencing needed changes will happen.

So many voices in our world are giving tacit or explicit consent to sexual relationships among young people. It is time for parents to learn from my friend. Do not allow your child to be sexually active. Will him to see the need to reserve sex for marriage. Teach him how to sublimate his sexual energies and to practice self-control.

■

YOUNG ADULTS

Perhaps your child is already beyond your healthy authority. He is not willing to listen to or respect your opinions. If he is eighteen or older, you have no legal recourse. In that case, love him, build a bridge of friendship, and teach as many facts as you can. He may have to learn the difficult way from the pain of his mistakes.

Without rescuing your child from the curative force of reality, let her face the consequences. But be prepared to walk through the painful experiences with her. Through sharing pain, a child often will learn, belatedly but well, what she could not hear from you.

Ellen was a fairly obedient child until she turned seventeen. She discovered a friend had been able to move away from home and into a room with her boyfriend. It sounded like playing house to Ellen, so she, too, left home and moved into her boyfriend's home. There were no rules. She could go to school or not, work or not, have sex as she pleased. No one was the boss. She dropped out of school. When she became pregnant, the boyfriend abandoned her and his mother asked her to leave.

For a very long time, her pride kept Ellen trying to make it on her own. Her brokenhearted mother managed to avoid rescuing her, though occasionally they talked on the phone. Finally from a distant state came the call for help: Could her mom help her find a place to live or let her come home? When her mother saw her, she could sense the maturing that had occurred. Ellen was convinced that free living and free sex were not so free. She faced the fact that she could not take care of her child, and she gave it up for adoption into a loving home. She was ready to start over.

Few stories turn out so well. Some of Ellen's contemporaries stay in the category of the homeless. A few straighten out their lives and make it on their own. Some parents refuse to forgive and allow their prodigal children to come home. Each one must make a personal decision. My hope lies in the prevention of such rebellion by better early training, discipline, and bonding.

Here are some steps one mother took to help her wayward child back to a healthy lifestyle:

1. She took the grave risk of setting strict guidelines her daughter had to live by in order to stay at home.
2. When this young woman refused to accept and honor the rules, her mother required her to leave.
3. Through relatives and friends, the mother kept in touch over ensuing months. She learned, with great pain, that her child's lifestyle was destructive.
4. Mother sent word on occasion that she loved her daughter and that her original proposition was still in effect.
5. After nearly two years of living in highly abusive situations, her child decided the price of her sexual freedom was too high. She went home.
6. Mother welcomed her back, helped nurse her back to complete health, and finally saw her child become a success.

Rebellion

15

"What do you do," an anxious mother asked, "when a thirteen-year-old doesn't take punishment and would rather do without something [as a consequence] than do what she is told?" Further conversation with Nan revealed years of struggle with a stubborn child. In the past year she had become rebellious. As we explored Mom's expectations, they sounded fair. Bridget was to keep her room clean, help with dinner and dishes for half an hour in the evenings, and maintain average grades. Her bedtime and telephone and TV privileges were quite generous and close to those of her friends. Yet she refused to follow the rules or complete her tasks. She was a rebellious child who needed special help.

Parents may well question the difference between stubborn or strong-willed children and rebellious ones. The best points of distinction that I can give are these:

- Rebellious children function out of anger in nearly total opposition to their parents. Strong-willed children are more likely to have strong beliefs and the determination to hold out for them.
- Rebellious kids behave in ways that are destructive to themselves and their environment. Strong-willed kids are less likely to do so.
- Rebellious kids usually feel they are treated unfairly and their parents are too rigid, so some of their behaviors are done in retaliation. They also feel they have to rebel to gain any independence or selfhood. Strong-willed kids are more secure in their selfhood.

What Nan discovered was this—though her rules were not extremely demanding, the perfection she required and the angry, critical attitude she evidenced created the climate for rebellion.

It is impossible for anyone to get through life without submitting, at times, to an authority beyond her own. So the work of those parents was obviously yet to be done. Nan missed the crucial point in her question. It was not whether Bridget would accept punishment, but whether she would, finally, do what she was told.

■

THE KEY: PERSISTENCE

I asked Nan to explain to Bridget that she would have to do certain agreed-upon tasks. I emphasized the importance of having family discussions that resulted in adopting a few policies for family living. They needed to include responsibilities, acceptable ways to treat each other, and basic guidelines for structuring time and spending money.

Once those rules were understood, rewards for keeping them and consequences for breaking them were agreed upon. All that was left for Nan was to enforce the agreement. In a certain sense, Bridget's world would stop until she followed through with the assignment. It takes perseverance to stick with this plan because a strong-willed child may take hours or even days to decide to give in.

I make the same recommendations to you if you have a rebellious child. Here are some ideas to make giving in more bearable to a child:

- Stay calm and matter-of-fact, even friendly. You can do this by putting yourself in your child's place. Bridget struggled with giving in because she actually feared she was giving up her personhood. It seemed to her that Mom's will would engulf her.
- Explain that your child has a choice. She may do the required task or continue to live by the consequences she has agreed upon. You may even show how sorry you feel for her restrictions.
- Do not give in. If you relent once, the rebellion will become worse.
- Do not let your child's problem of rebelling become yours. When Bridget could make Nan upset, she knew she had won. Nan would fret and scold, but Bridget was in charge. If you stay in charge, both parent and child will be on the same team, but the parent is rightfully captain.

Once you have outlasted a rebellious child, subsequent times will become gradually easier. The first time you will be tempted to give up and resort to other measures. I trust you will persist until you discover how well this approach works.

■

INDEPENDENCE BEYOND SAFE BOUNDS

Bridget's rebellion was annoying and even worrisome to her mother. But Gilbert's was really frightening. He was born to parents who were perfectionists. They had every area of family living planned and organized to the last closet and drawer. Their clothes closets and linen cupboards were color coordinated; every towel and washcloth was folded precisely and stacked evenly.

The exactness had penetrated their family rules, which were thoroughly written in outlines. Nothing they could imagine was left uncovered by the minutest details of their family life.

The problem was that Gilbert was the second and middle child. Furthermore, he was easygoing by nature. Complying with his parents' rigidity and excessive demands was too much for him. He began to push his curfew a few minutes. Of course, he was lectured and grounded for a few days, but to him, putting up with the consequences was worth having the extra time of freedom. He began, at fourteen, to feel a bit independent.

He discovered he could watch TV programs he wanted if he stayed awake until his parents were asleep. He deliberately chose ones his parents forbade. Late at night he could also talk to friends—not the best students or most law-abiding citizens, as a rule. Bit by bit, Gilbert found more ways to deceive his parents by doing more things, including using alcohol and some drugs. He had felt so strangled by his parents' rigid rules that he made certain his choices were opposite of their requirements. As so commonly happens in rebellion, Gilbert went against the decisions he would have liked to make to doubly ensure that he was free of them.

It was inevitable that Gilbert began to feel guilty. Perhaps due to his deep-down wish to change, he became more careless about his habits. His parents discovered his harmful behaviors, and a major struggle began. They did everything they could to make him return to their way of life. Gilbert left home and lived with friends for a time; his destructive habits worsened.

Finally with considerable professional help, his caring parents began to understand that they would need to give in a little if they hoped to salvage any relationship with their son. Because of their deeply rooted habits and rigid thinking, being flexible to any degree was heroic for them. But to their credit, they tried. Gratefully, Gilbert began to give up bits of his misbehaviors, and the bridge back into his family was built slowly.

Gilbert's problems were due to full-blown rebelliousness. The risks were far more dangerous than those of Bridget, who was resisting her parents' authority. Truly rebellious kids may carry their actions to any degree, some more and others less serious. Many young people can find no other way to become free of overly strict, supercontrolling parents.

ON THE STREET

Meg showed up in an emergency room of a large city hospital. My friend, a physician, told me her story. She was only fifteen but looked thirty. Dressed in skimpy, tight leather clothing, she looked like the street person she was. Her jewelry was a mass of heavy metal chains, and her makeup masked her youthful face.

My friend was so distressed by the silent screams of the girl's life that she felt she could hardly touch her to examine her. Fortunately, my doctor friend said, she was called to the telephone. While out of the room, she tried to think more warmly about the hardened young rebel. She even prayed for God's help because she knew she couldn't deal with what she sensed was hurting her patient.

Upon her return, she managed to feel quite different. My friend thoroughly checked the girl physically and found her to have a serious venereal disease. She was also addicted to cocaine. For at least six months she had been living on the streets earning money by prostituting herself.

The story Meg poured out was heartbreaking. Her parents had been divorced for five years. She rarely saw her father, who seemed to have no interest in her at all. As a matter of fact, she revealed, she had hardly seen her mother for the year before she left home. Mom worked nights and went out with a series of men in her spare time. Her mom had started to drink a lot, and she yelled at Meg or sat drunk and sobbing when she was at home.

Meg felt her mom was relieved when she left a note telling her she wouldn't be back. She was lonely and scared but desperate and proud. Never would she admit life on the streets was too much for her, so day by day she made herself act more calloused and tough. She became pretty good at her role!

Before parting from Meg, my friend sat down, pulled her onto her lap, and hugged her while she sobbed like the child she was. The doctor did all she could to provide help for the young woman. I do not know the end of her story, but I know many variations of her sad saga, some with eventually happy endings, but many with tragic and even fatal outcomes.

Meg's story is a true one, and she looked and acted like an extremely rebellious teenager. But she is actually one of those people who behaved like a rebel while the underlying dynamics were very different from those of a true rebel. Meg had tested the boundaries and rules all her life, finding them missing most of the time. In her almost desperate search for some evidence that her mother cared about her, she found only that Mom was relieved of responsibility and free from arguments when she finally ran away.

It is of extreme importance that you understand the difference in the causes of rebellious behaviors versus true rebellion. Rebellion, as was stated earlier, is related to parents' perceived rigidity, control, and unfairness. The look-alike of rebellious-type behavior is caused by the opposite extreme in parenting. This extreme has too few limits and, at best, inconsistent enforcement. Children of these parents behave in dangerous, wild ways, but they long for their parents to care enough, to be wise enough, and to be strong enough to stop them. I will remind you of this vital truth as often as possible!

■
GETTING HIS WAY

Lester was a popular guy of sixteen. He was always ready for a prank and good for a joke that would elicit laughter, so it was no wonder his peers enjoyed his company. He didn't like to study, however, and barely made the grades that allowed him to get his high-school diploma. He began to smoke during his junior year in high school, sneaked out to see movies at times, and got by with some minor law breaking without serious consequences. He was on his way to serious rebellion.

And that rebellion was understandable. His parents were extremely rigid, angry, punitive, and guilt producing. The whole family had to be in church for every scheduled event. There was no dancing or skating because the places where such activities could be found were not very nice. No one could play cards because cards were used in gambling. No one could attend movies because they were bad influences. (I must agree that many are exactly that!) The list of don'ts far outweighed the few dos that could have been fun. Even school sports events were taboo if they fell on a church night.

Bit by bit Lester established his independence from his unyielding parents. At last they realized they could no longer control their son. They did love him and kept communication open, and he slowly reestablished a relationship with them.

Only then did Lester discover a basic fact. He, like most rebels, was doing things he really didn't want to do at all. His smoking, for example, became his way of telling his controlling parents, "You can't boss everything I do!" The other risky behaviors, too, he relinquished, one by one. In the end, his values were remarkably close to those of his parents.

How sad that they didn't understand! If only they had been a bit more flexible, if only they had not lectured so sternly and punished so harshly, their son could have tolerated their rules and adopted their values without the high risk of his rebellious years.

■

UNDERSTANDING REBELLION

These examples are about real people. Let's review them briefly.

■ Who's Right?

Bridget rebelled against her mother's harsh, condemning attitude and rigid perfectionism. In addition, her father joined the mother in the unbending competition for power. The family had a double problem of rebellion and a basic power struggle. Even though she was outnumbered (and probably *because* she was), Bridget intensified her efforts to outpower her parents' authority.

They finally realized they were part of the problem and employed gentler, more loving methods. When

Bridget could feel their love more clearly than their frustration, her rebellion subsided. Their love motivated her to want to please them.

The dictionary definition of *rebellion* is "resisting authority" or "opposing any controls." This makes the rebel look like *the* problem. But I trust you can see that parents are also part of the difficulty. When Bridget was given some control and was allowed some choices, she could tolerate the authority she did need from her parents.

■ No Other Way Out

Gilbert was another rebel. He tried to adapt to his parents' excessively rigid standards and unbending attitude. It seemed to him that he would be overwhelmed by the odds stacked against him. When such a life became unbearable to him, he could see no other way out. He began secret rebellion, which became overt and put him at risk.

In today's Western culture, permissiveness has become much more the norm. There are, however, a few families who practice the rigid, often harsh lifestyle of Gilbert's parents. No doubt, the evident flexibility of his friends' parents made his life all the more unbearable for Gilbert.

In spite of the rebelliousness it often creates, I believe we need more parental authority. It is easy to lessen the rules, from the youth's perspective. But it is extremely difficult for most young people to accept more rules and authority when they have had excessive freedom.

The answer to the prevention and the alleviation of

rebellion like Gilbert's is to expand the limits and reduce the rules. Include the teen or child in regular discussions of family policies and issues of concern. Heed her ideas and respect her feelings. You will likely be surprised by how quickly she will return to cooperating with the family.

Don't forget, however, that you as a parent need to exercise veto power when necessary. Set the big boundaries, and teach your child to exercise individuality and practice making wise decisions within these limits. The more good you see and reflect to your child, the more likely he'll be to live up to it. You can often prevent serious rebellion.

■ Too Much of a Good Thing

Lester's problems were much like Gilbert's. In his case, however, the parents added another component to their overly strict, unbending attitudes. They used their religious beliefs and church activities as exclusive determiners of their entire lifestyle. Faith in God is at the top of my values, but I believe God can be honored in all parts of life. Allowing Lester to take a more active role in his school would have brought balance in his life. Had he been able to take part in the wholesome activities of his school, one can predict he would have been less likely to rebel. He needed peer interaction and a chance to develop some skills that would build confidence.

■

COPING WITH REBELLION

Rebellion comes in several forms and from as many causes. Once you know the basis, ways of coping with it become much clearer. Here are some guidelines:

- If the rebellion is based on power struggles between two strong-willed people, back off. Avoid setting up a win-lose situation. Make as few rules as possible, stick with them tenaciously, and by waiting out the time, allow the agreed-upon consequences to motivate your strong-willed child to comply.
- The hurting child needs comfort, reassurances, and safety. If you are a parent whose needs currently outstrip your resources, seek help. Through a church, a professional counselor, relatives, or friends, get your needs met. Then you will be able to help your child. Books are very useful, and by all means include the greatest book of all—the Bible.
- If your child is a truly classic rebel due to excessively rigid and numerous rules, try to become more flexible. Most serious rebellion occurs in the adolescent years. By then, a young person needs to learn some lessons on his own, even if that means he makes some mistakes. Try to prevent disasters, but give your teen enough freedom to experience some natural consequences. The results of the mistakes will teach him far more effectively than a

thousand rules. The more lovingly *and* firmly you deal with a rebel, the better he will learn.

- Finally, if you believe you have a rebellious child but you are quite lenient, consider the possibility you are too permissive. A child searching for boundaries often carries out that search through acting out. She wants excessive freedom, but most of all, she is trying to find out how far you will let her go. Find and hold on to some boundaries, working carefully with your child. These limits should expand only in proportion to your child's demonstrated sense of responsibility.

Even a rebellious child can change into a responsible independent adult.

Sometimes rebellious children have a core of strength inside them that is healthy. They rarely understand clearly why they rebel, and they simply react against the pain they experience from too tight reins or neglect. But as you discover the cause, you will be able to form the balance, maintain the appropriate boundaries, and promote the healing of your child's pain. Then your family can grow in harmony and love.

16

The Difficult Teen

Some people feel that all teens are difficult and, at times, unbearable. I must confess that I understand that feeling. But for some thirty years, I have worked with troubled teens, and I have learned to see through their offensive attitudes and behaviors to the wonderful people they actually are. Sometimes the most profoundly troubled young people have been the most honest, insightful, and caring members of their families.

What happens in the lives of adolescents to make them seem difficult? Let's explore the developmental stages prior to adolescence. We can understand what may go wrong that results in difficulty and how to prevent or repair it.

■
_____

THE ANTECEDENTS OF ADOLESCENCE

Developmentally, the major task of teens is to become productive, functional, and independent
adults. This task demands a complex and rapidly changing interaction among teens, parents, teachers, and employers.

Many people do not realize that much earlier in life,
there is a precursor to adolescence—that is, the age of
two to three years. Many people call that developmental
stage the terrible twos. At that tender age, children first
stretch for independence; it's to a different degree, of
course, from the independence sought by teens. It
makes sense that this universal reach of two-year-olds
and teens is not only necessary but healthy.

The problems that emerge during these stages are related to parents' lack of knowledge about them. Parents
are threatened by their children's separation from them.
They feel that the children no longer love or need them
and that they could be out of a job, so to speak!

At age two, children begin to master both physical and
relationship changes that set them well on the long journey to adulthood. They must learn to talk and communicate their needs more specifically than by crying. They
must give up the security of diapers to sit on cold potties.
They usually give up the bottle, breast, and pacifier, and
they must learn to feed themselves. They want to explore every nook and cranny of the house, feeling and
tasting everything they can reach.

During these months, parents' responses to their children set much of the stage for their adolescent years. Wise parents are sympathetic and understanding about many things two-year-olds have to give up or lose. They allow slow motion in making the necessary changes, comforting the grief that accompanies all losses, but holding firm the required boundaries to protect the children. Good parents encourage exploring, adventuring with them, and provide protective boundaries within which children may safely function. They structure the children's days, teach the rudiments of a sense of responsibility, and help children feel good about themselves and the parents.

The end of this era should result in children's feeling safe in their environment, worthwhile in their being, and valued and loved in their relationships. They are ready to move on to ever more complex developmental tasks.

In the preschool years, children enter a delightful period of growth. They are able to entertain themselves independently for various periods of time. They demonstrate a charming degree of creativity and imagination. They have resolved most of their grief over the losses of the twos and are beginning to think about some abstract concepts. Many four-year-olds, for example, wonder about God and heaven. They may know that Grandma died and went to heaven, so they wonder if their pet that died also went to heaven.

From about age six to age twelve, children are busy growing physically, mentally, and socially. They are learning a sense of duty and should discover what happens when they fall short in being responsible. Successful parents set up policies, establish consequences, and allow natural consequences to go into effect. By these methods, children are being prepared for the independence of adolescence.

PREADOLESCENCE

Physically and socially, children have been developing more and more precociously in recent years. Puberty may be well advanced by age nine or ten and commonly is established by age eleven or twelve.

Schools have pushed eleven- or twelve-year-old youngsters (sixth graders) into a middle school setting. They lose the attachment to one primary teacher and pass from room to room and person to person all day long. I have counted as many as nine separate individuals to whom a child must adjust every day.

In a precociously adult setting (a middle school being much like a high school), children quickly pick up teen behaviors. In the past few years, as a consultant, I have been called to interview ten children who were explicitly sexually involved with peers. They were all sixth graders, and each one was striving to establish himself or herself as a sophisticated young adult. I was not able to evaluate their partners, but the children I saw named several other children with whom they were sexually involved.

The premature independence of preadolescents creates more problems and feeds the difficulties of adolescence. When children grow up too soon and behave independently of adult authority too much, a tragic deficit occurs in their development. They never really complete their developmental stage. Like a plant without an adequate root system, they topple in the winds of change. Because their dependency needs aren't met, these children substitute peers or other acquaintances for their absent parents to meet their needs for security. They attach to each other in unhealthy ways and degrees, increasing a vicious circle of dependency that cannot result in truly mature individuals.

Preadolescents need to have extensive teaching about their physical development and their sexuality. This teaching must include a sense of responsibility and respect toward others and themselves. Their parents and teachers are vital role players in this educational function.

Families, schools, and the entire community need to form a collaborative team working together for children. They must communicate clearly and regularly regarding children's strengths and weaknesses, assets and liabilities, if children are to receive the help they need to become healthy independent adults.

■

PORTALS OF ADOLESCENCE

At fifteen, Judy was an energetic, bright ninth grader. She was beginning to show the signs of problems—she took an occasional drink of alcohol from friends' supplies, she smoked a cigarette now and then, allegedly pilfered from a friend's supply, and she was not always to be found where she said she was going.

Judy's mother realized that she had been too busy, not available enough to her child. So she accepted her responsibility for the need to change. She had been overly trusting and had given her basically conscientious child too much freedom.

Major changes took place in the family. Mother rearranged her schedule so she would be available when Judy arrived home from school. She had cookies and milk or a snack available, and the two sat together to build a better relationship and stop the misbehaviors. Knowing she, too, had done wrong, Judy was pretty defensive. She answered her mom's questions in monosyllables, and at the first possible moment, she escaped to the privacy of her room.

One day Judy had had enough. She arose to her full four feet ten inches and delivered a shocking blow to her mom's psyche. With blue eyes blazing and fists clenched, she blurted out the pent-up rage of several weeks: "Mom, you're so smart! You oughtta know I'm fifteen; I'm not a five-year-old kindergartner. Don't treat me like one!" She stomped off, leaving her mother in agony and tears.

But Mom didn't give up. Instead of reprimanding her daughter for her rudeness, she contemplated the girl's message. As is common with teenagers, Judy had accurately perceived the situation.

Mother thought hard and prayed earnestly for wisdom with which to help her child. She realized that Judy was not a kindergartner. She was indeed fifteen, not five! The next consideration logically was this: "If Judy were an adult friend and not my child, how would I relate with her differently?" Mother knew the answer very well! She would not quiz a friend about her daily events. Instead, she would chat interactively, sharing her life with her friend.

Mother knew that she needed to continue to spend time with her daughter, but she knew even better the use of their time would have to be changed. The next day over chips and sodas, there were no questions. Judy was delightedly taken off guard when her mother began to describe a poignant event in which she had been involved that day. She had not quite completed her narrative when Judy interrupted with a question and a comment. Before either of them realized it, they were chatting away freely, like good friends do.

That day, Mom and Judy became more friend and friend and less mother and daughter. It was Judy's day to pass through the portals of childhood to young womanhood. Certainly, there were stormy days ahead. Mom reverted occasionally to old habits. Judy acknowledged that she sometimes slipped into childish behaviors. But both of them kept working out the problems.

Today Judy and her mother are partners. They often reminisce about the days of Judy's transition from girl to woman.

∎ A Traditional Gateway

In the ancient traditions of the Jewish faith, there is a built-in gateway through adolescence. At the age of twelve, Jewish boys and girls enter a rigorous year-long course of study. They give up the late Saturday morning sleep-ins and limit Friday night slumber parties. By nine o'clock on Saturday, they are in the synagogue. They read and study together their Torah, their many religious celebrations, and their profound beliefs. Their families are also involved, and the year ends in a festive celebration called a Bar or Bas Mitzvah. Everyone knows, within the context of the Jewish traditions, this young person has become an adult. The ceremony takes place on or about the person's thirteenth birthday.

What a wonderful concept and tradition the Mitzvah rites are! There is a familiar and well-defined difference in expectations of young people before and afterward.

I know and love lots of Jewish friends, and none of them would state that their thirteen-year-olds have absolute freedom after their Mitzvah celebration. Yet there is little serious rebellion among the adolescents in Jewish families. After discussing this fact at length, I see two reasons. First, since early teens are respected as young adults, they do not need to rebel. Second, the rules and authority in Jewish traditions rest with the family. Parents and the entire Jewish community unite in respect to providing guidance and protection for their teens.

Few Christian denominations have such a ceremonial transition from childhood to adulthood. It would seem that the confirmation classes many churches conduct are comparable. In my experience, however, these classes deal solely with religious teaching and spiritual commitment. They do not end with the overall graduation of teens to adult status.

Judy's mother was pushed into building a gateway for her. And perhaps it would work well if each family developed an individual celebration of that entry into young adulthood. Be creative and find your own ideas, but realize the immense importance of inviting your child to enter your grown-up world.

■

SYMPTOMS OF TROUBLE

There are several symptoms of teenagers who are in trouble. Some of them are transient and occur universally in one degree or another. When these symptoms are intense enough to cause concern in parents and teachers and put the teens at risk, they indicate the need for help. Furthermore, let me remind you, if they are signs of serious difficulty, they will last at least two weeks. Though there may well be more than this concise list, these are the universal symptoms.

■ Moodiness

Due in part to physical changes such as puberty and rapid growth spurts, adolescents suffer from dour moods. In girls, these often are worsened by premenstrual tension. Often moods are related to social or academic problems. If an adolescent was born with a temperament in which moods lay on the negative end of the spectrum, adolescent moodiness can be severe.

■ Withdrawal

Sometimes adolescents express their moodiness openly and even rudely to their friends and families. These are bigmouthed difficult kids. Others run to their rooms and slam their doors, isolating themselves. When parents approach their rooms, the teens are likely to yell and reject contact. Interestingly enough, most withdrawn teens tell me privately they yearn for their parents to respond to them, yet they *seem* to resist it. Parents, remember, need to be strong enough, wise enough, and caring enough to overcome and outwait these periods of withdrawal.

In occasional cases, withdrawal means a teen runs away. Once in a while this action is due to abuse at home and expresses the self-protective instinct of a youth. In many other situations, however, running away is a test of the extent of parents' caring or true rebellion against extreme rigidity.

■ Conduct Disorders

From skipping class to abusing chemicals, most teens are going to test authority. When their parents have been either extremely permissive or excessively rigid, they will do a number of things to change the situation. We have discussed the dynamics of the rebellious child. Pathological conduct is the symptom of this problem: refusing to do jobs, allowing schoolwork to fail, choosing friends who are bad influences, or becoming actively involved in lying, stealing, cheating, sexual acting out, fighting, abusing drugs and/or alcohol, speeding, and committing countless acts that are either illegal or ill advised.

Unfortunately, few parents see these actions as symptoms so they punish; they fail to understand and build bridges. Don't misunderstand! These actions are dangerous and must be stopped. But concurrently, help for the family usually makes an immense difference in the rapidity with which positive changes occur.

The child who acts out may be trying to save the family in some way. Charlotte was a tall, slender teen, except for her abdomen—swollen with her eight-month pregnancy. She readily confided that her parents had never gotten along well. Over time, she had discovered that a crisis would unite her parents for a while. Through the years, Charlotte had deliberately but cleverly created crises, consciously trying to save her parents' marriage and her family.

■ Grief and Depression

Teens, like two-year-olds, grieve over many losses. They may lose male and female friends, lose jobs, experience the divorce of parents, fail to reach certain goals in school and sports endeavors, and finally face the increasing awareness that they must enter an adult world —soon. It's small wonder that teens become depressed.

Depressed teens experience anger, sadness, guilt, anxiety, worry, fear, and a profound sense of helplessness. In many teens, depression becomes fatal.

Parents need to be aware of these signs of potential suicide:

- Clear changes occur in school performance and behaviors.
- Observable changes occur in physical functioning. Sleeping becomes excessive or difficult. Eating habits reveal either excessive consumption of food or a loss of appetite.
- Social functioning suffers. Hygiene and grooming deteriorate. The teen may dress in black or drab colors.
- Withdrawal becomes extreme, and moods are severely negative.

- The person gives away cherished possessions or drafts a written will.
- A suicidal person sees no tomorrow; the person despairs of things in life ever becoming better.
- These symptoms must last at least two weeks, and a majority of them must be present during this time if these symptoms constitute true major depression.

Any teen with four or more of these symptoms needs a professional evaluation. If even one symptom is severe, an evaluation is wise. Don't take a chance on your teen's life.

■ Emotional Disorders

Besides depression, teens may experience several emotional disorders. They may develop anxiety and serious fears such as concern over war, famine, and other global affairs.

Sylvia is an example of the compound problem that an emotional disorder and a behavioral aberration can create. Sylvia had been a model child and student. It was in the spring of her senior year in high school that she first evidenced some problems. Along with two close friends, she entered a big department store to shop. During the course of the next hour, she stole three expensive items. Her parents and friends were stunned, and the store manager was furious!

As a matter of fact, Sylvia was horrified! As she began to talk about her shoplifting, she also revealed her anxiety. In only a few weeks she would be out of the shelter of school, facing an adult world. She felt totally inadequate to cope with holding down a job, managing her time and money, and in a while moving away from home. She was acting out the painful anxiety she felt. Never again did Sylvia steal. She learned she didn't have to do everything at once, and her mother reassured her that she would help her take every one of those first adult steps.

Anxiety has many manifestations. It is the expression of inner conflict and confusion. The teen wants to do certain things but fears he can't or knows they may be wrong. He wants to please adults but also wants to be his own boss. She has gone with Bruce for several months, but now she'd like to get to know Ken. Teens especially are blessed with such conflicts, but they have inadequate experience or wisdom with which to solve the problems. Furthermore, they are too proud to admit they need help. A part of separating from parents is believing parents really don't know much anyway. So teens often feel isolated with their ambivalences.

Anxiety may quickly mushroom into panic attacks or phobias. These are manifested by a rapid heart rate, some degree of difficulty breathing, and great muscle tension. Often there are headaches and stomachaches, but the worst symptom is a feeling of impending doom, a sense that some dreadful thing may happen. In my experience, conscientious, hardworking teens are the ones who have these attacks. They seem to fear that their very best efforts are not enough, and they see no sure resource for help.

Some young people learn to focus on the physical signs of anxiety, and they may become hypochondriacs. Much of this tendency is temporary. The real but emotionally based physical pain is easier to express and gains more attention and help than the emotional state of anxiety.

■ Oppositional or Defiant Disorders

As a part of establishing independence, most teens become, at least temporarily, argumentative. It doesn't matter what the adults around them say, they are going to oppose the idea. When parents or teachers fail to understand the cause of this behavior, they are likely to try to force teens into seeing their point and agreeing with them.

A teen who acts defiant is really trying to establish her independence. She fears her parents are controlling her too much, and she has to make them see *her* point.

DEALING WITH THE DIFFICULT TEEN

Let's get the basic facts about helping the difficult teen and then a few specifics.

■ Foster Independence

Since the big job of a teen is to learn how to become independent, your biggest task as a parent is to help that happen. Yet you must keep some protective boundaries. My recipe for success in this area is to think *with* your teen, not *for* him. Help him practice the SOCC formula:

- *S*ize up the situation in focus.
- List all the *o*ptions possible.
- Select one *c*hoice out of all those listed.

- Allow the consequences of that choice to be felt but never say, "I told you so!"

■ Expand the Boundaries

But don't destroy boundaries. A teen must learn to make sensible decisions, but she still needs your bottom line held intact. Guide the thinking of your adolescent by asking questions and sharing your thoughts. Only when a bad choice could be permanently damaging should you plant your feet firmly. Renew your information about your teen's inborn temperament to help you know how best to put your foot down—for example, wait it out with a stubborn teen, gently teach a compliant one, and muster every bit of energy and help you can for a defiant one!

■ Show Respect

If you expect to get respect, show it for your teen. Throughout this book, there are examples of parents who have eased or intensified a conflict with their teens depending on how well the parents responded to the teens. Judy's mom allowed some disrespect from Judy at the moment, but she gained a lifetime of mutual respect by taking time to communicate later her respect for Judy's frustration.

■ Listen

Stop talking and listen actively to your teen. If the respect has been established, you will find listening easier. Avoid acting as if your teen is a child, and never discount or ridicule his ideas. You may disagree to the end, but allowing a teen to express ideas keeps communication alive. I express my opinion and experience, listen to those of the teen, and then suggest we both think about all of the ideas and talk about the matter later. Once I learned to do that, I discovered that a teen's sometimes foolish-sounding statements had real merit in them. What may begin as a superficial effort to give a teen a voice can grow into surprisingly real respect.

■ Share Yourself

Choose your moments carefully and your words even more wisely. Never try to show her up by making yourself look heroic. But do show her that you can to some degree understand her because you lived through a similar episode. Talk briefly about your childhood and adolescence. Share some of your failures and disappointments as well as your successes. Perhaps you, too, failed to make the varsity team! At times you feel discouraged or get in a mood. You know a bit about how she feels.

■

LET'S GET SPECIFIC

For each expression of teenage problems, here are some suggestions. Use them mainly as a springboard for your creative ideas.

■ Moodiness

I suggest finding out in a moment of calm how long your teen needs to be alone while in a bad mood. Allow enough time, but keep an end point in mind. Remember the secrets of my troubled teens—they all wished Mom or Dad had come to them. Use these steps:

1. Express comfort and simple understanding: "I'm sorry you're upset."
2. Offer to listen: "If you need a sounding board, here I am, a great listener."
3. Offer to help: "Can you think of anything I can do to see you through this difficulty?" If there is no answer, suggest something appropriate.
4. Suggest a diversion: "Dinner will be ready in half an hour," or "There's a great program on TV at eight o'clock. I'd love to have you watch it with me."
5. Give a brief touch (depending on your child's wishes), and promise to be back.

■ Withdrawal

As with moodiness, allow some time off the topic or even away from the family. But always return—not with harshness or punishment. Offer caring, help, and hope for the future. How much better this approach works than an angry voice demanding, "You talk to me right now, young man! And show me respect!" Just like the tiny two-year-old, the obstreperous teen is going to silently say, "No!" If your child has been a runaway, seek professional help. That risky behavior may endanger a child's safety.

■ Conduct Disorders

Chemical abuse, school failures, and illegal acts are serious symptoms. The best you can do is to try to talk with your teen to see if he has any idea why he would put himself at risk. Be genuine in trying to work with him to determine what would more effectively meet his need instead of misbehaving. If he cannot help in this search, I strongly recommend counseling. An objective, non-threatening helper will usually provide the answers few families can find alone.

■ Grief and Depression

You can detect these in your teen by watching her. Her downcast face, drooping shoulders, and lethargic demeanor shout their message of sadness. Listen to that, and think. Grief is often the result of relatively minor losses in teens who are moody anyway. Losing an *A* or a loyal friend may seem insignificant to you, but it isn't to your teen. A teen who is sad needs a caring heart and a shoulder to cry on. The problem is, she is pretty choosy about which shoulder and heart she can trust. Offer yours, but don't feel angry or rejected if your teen selects a friend instead. In fact, you may suggest someone to your teen. Just be available, interested but not invasive, and supportive.

■ Emotional Disorders

If your teen's emotional problem is anxiety, worry, or fear, you almost certainly need to seek counseling. These painful feelings often are accompanied by guilt—

real or imagined. The guilt is commonly unconscious and usually is due not to really bad actions but to a sense of not being good enough. Occasionally, a parent and a teen are open and sensitive enough to determine some of the underlying problems. If so, and if the family can work them out, that's a wonderful outcome.

■ Oppositional or Defiant Disorders

In a teen, this problem is the equivalent of the strong-willed child, discussed earlier. The best approach is to stop opposing this young person. The usual scenario demonstrates that the teen has a parent with the identical problem. Opposing each other does not work, and if you have a defiant adolescent, you've already discovered that. With a teen, you will find the most successful solution in working toward friendship, adult-to-adult communication, and thoughtful, reasonable problem solving.

■

GET SOME HELP

Professional counseling can be not only comforting and helpful but also lifesaving. So do not allow your pride or fear to rob you of that asset if you believe you need it.

Here are some indicators that your teen and you need professional help:

- The signs of serious depression and possible suicide listed previously are persistently or recurrently present.

- Your teen's misbehaviors are endangering her health and education and creating grave unhappiness.
- Your best efforts to provide guidance and encouragement are not helping.
- Teachers, friends, or relatives, more objective than parents can be, see signs of serious difficulty.

In selecting a counselor, seek someone who understands family dynamics and will include you in the process of helping your teen. Find someone who respects your values and beliefs, and who can relate comfortably with teenagers. I recommend asking your minister, your family doctor, or your child's school nurse or counselor for a referral resource.

There are other sources of help, too. Trusted relatives can give you feedback that may open your insight and improve your handling of your teen. Having a brief "cooling off" period when tensions rise can be advisable. Ask a family member to invite your teen for a weekend away. Or you go somewhere! You will be able to see issues much more clearly when you are together again.

Many times a clergyperson or a volunteer at your house of worship can be your support. Be honest with the person about your weak spots and your concerns. Never put your child in an unfavorable light, but don't try to hide the problems. Simply and clearly ask for the specific helps you and your teen need.

Many adolescents make special friends with neighbors, teachers, or employers. Some parents become jealous of the attachments. It does pay to be certain these adults are healthy people who will not use or abuse your teen. Make friends with them. And then be grateful for the supplemental parenting they can offer. I'm convinced many of these helping people are guardian angels.

Finally, and most important of all, pray. The power of this spiritual force is immeasurable. God loves you and your child far more than we could ever describe. Trust God's wisdom to guide you, His love to inspire you, and His strength to empower you! Your reliance on Him will make the ultimate difference.

17

Understanding
the Difficulty

The *difficult person* is defined by *Webster's Dictionary* as "hard to satisfy, persuade, etc." The noun *difficulty* adds "obstacle or objection, trouble, a disagreement or quarrel." The root words literally translate "not easy."

Those of you with a difficult child can certainly validate these words! You know about the obstacle a stubborn child can erect in the family's path. The quarreling of a rebellious child and the trouble caused by a lazy child are difficulties shared by many families.

In her book *Toxic Parents*, Dr. Susan Foward studiously delineates how the problems of parents invade and influence the developing lives of their children. She reiterates the ancient biblical truth in Numbers 14:18: "He by no means clears the guilty, visiting the iniquity of the fathers on the children to the third and fourth generation."

It is unlikely that parents decide to abuse their children. In fact, parents will fiercely protect their children from harm. Yet, by all reports, many parents *do* abuse their children. Reports range from 750,000 to a million verified cases of physical abuse of minor children annually in America. As already written, emotional abuse cannot be adequately defined. Most of us can recall episodes of severe emotional pain inflicted by our parents. Sometimes this pain makes wayward children change, but often the pain emerges from parents who are passing on the pain inflicted by their parents and grandparents.

Much as we hate it, we must face the fact that a great many difficult children are the products of Dr. Foward's described toxic parents. The good news is this—no matter what the abuse, its damage can be healed and its transmission to future generations stopped. Just become unafraid to face your mistakes and correct them. This sounds simple, and of course, it isn't. But the hard work it takes is worth it all.

In our hurried, and often harried, world, we are aware that people of all ages can be difficult. In their interpersonal reactions and communications, a hidden problem may have a harmful effect on their relationships. Difficult employers or bosses are all too well known. Between coworkers, conflicts can create an unhealthy climate. Among neighbors, mistrust and retaliation are too common. Any serious difficulty is more than likely to set off a vicious circle of actions and reactions that result in pain and destruction.

Unfortunately, families are not exempt from weighty problems. For example, a teenager sexually molested his younger cousin. He promised her protection if she would submit and ridicule if she ever dared to tell. His damaging actions and words haunted the girl over her shortened life span. Out of her false guilt and helplessness grew the despair that convinced her she should die.

A father's gruff words, "You'll never make it in baseball, Son!" became a negative prediction that short-circuited a promising career. He almost made it to a major league team, but in the inner core of his being, those discouraging words persisted: "You'll never make it, Son!" And he never did.

An accomplished opera star anxiously awaited a performance in a small town. As she nervously paced the floor in the wings, she spoke of her critical, implacable mother in the audience. All of her life she had yearned for her mother's "Bravo! Well done!" But those words had yet to be heard. Once again, she feared, she would hear, "Those high notes were just not very clear, my dear!"

Difficult parents are plentiful in our stress-filled world. They abuse their children while professing love for them, and the abuse occurs in many forms. Physical overpunishment is frighteningly common. Verbal abuse is rampant. If you doubt this truth, stand in any grocery store or shopping area, and you'll observe it. Sexual abuse allegedly scars one out of three girls and one in four boys. One study in 1985 revealed that 27 percent of American women and 16 percent of men were sexual abuse victims. That would total about 38 million people nationwide.

Neglect leaves countless kids feeling lost and unworthy. But neglect is rarely reported, and no reliable studies are available that begin to tally its tragic damage.

Whether abuse is perpetrated by parents or allowed by them, it is equally damaging. Children brought up in such an environment suffer clearly defined injuries. They have low self-esteem and are seriously deficient in self-confidence. They often punish themselves for the false guilt abusive situations impart. Almost universally, they endure feelings of inadequacy, failure, and fear. Many of them compensate for the painful emotions by focusing on one area in which they do fairly well. Others become bullies, antagonizing friends and families alike, perpetuating their family pattern. Indeed, difficult parents help create difficult kids, who in turn pass on this harmful habit.

Research has revealed that from 20 to 50 percent of psychiatric hospital patients were victims of child abuse. As many as 61 percent of adolescents with the dual diagnoses of chemical addiction and another psychiatric diagnosis were previously abused.

If you have a difficult child, however, take courage! The child's behavior may not be your fault after all. In fact, searching for someone to blame seems to me a waste of energy. Recognizing family habits or realizing your mistakes can certainly facilitate the discovery of a way to get through to the child and overcome the problem. But focusing on faults, mistakes, and blame creates more resentment.

When it's *no* one's fault, then, why are there so many families struggling with a difficult child? What set up the habits that cause inconvenience or downright anguish for the rest of the family members? Every conceivable cause has been studied. Experts offer a range of explanations but few specific answers.

Many facets of family life, woven together, create the environment of a difficult child. In turn, the child's temperament enters into further weaving.

■
_____

INBORN FACTORS

The majority of you parents have never abused your child. The next section is for you. I trust these explanations will alleviate all of your false guilt, help you profoundly understand your child and, best of all, help him overcome his difficulty.

Researchers over many years explored the inborn qualities of life that add up to a child's temperament. Their studies showed clear differences among babies in newborn nurseries. Drs. Stella Chess and Alexander Thomas initiated this brilliant and tedious research, and their findings are most enlightening. They categorized nine areas in which there were measurable differences among newborn babies. Furthermore, the babies' mothers were included in the studies. They were evaluated for more or less intensity of the temperamental traits.

As you can well imagine, very different traits for mothers and infants sometimes caused trouble. If mothers (or primary caregivers) were strongly weighted in one direction and children were equally intense in the opposite direction, conflicts of some sort were predictable.

These studies were begun at birth, but they continued over decades. A significant number of families were tracked over a span of three or more decades. The results of this research revealed that many parent-child conflicts began at birth but continued at least for the duration of the child's growing-up years.

It is certain that many difficult children are born with extreme sensitivity to changes in their environment. They also react intensely to these changes. When these characteristics endure for years, you can see how problematic the situation becomes. Add to this, one or both parents who are quite different from such a child, and the entire picture becomes clear. Yet there are answers.

Let's think about these nine characteristics of babies and mothers.

■ Activity Level

Many mothers have told me that even before birth, they can tell a big difference in the activity level of their babies. A mother who has lots of energy and loves to engage in many activities may have major problems with a laid-back, slow-moving child. This mother may become impatient and irritable with a placid child. The disapproval her child feels and the child's own frustration can cause life to get off to a conflictual start. Neither Mom nor child intends to act angry or feel resentful, but the facts of their differences are real. They do not feel harmonious.

■ Distractibility

Colin can sit for an entire afternoon putting construction blocks together in an infinite variety of ways. His mother gets fidgety just watching him. She does great at housecleaning, but she hates to sit and type. She is pleased when the doorbell and the telephone ring at the same time. She loves excitement, and she seems to be on the go constantly. She can't comprehend Colin's ability to sit still. She wants him to spring up when she calls and bounce along with her wherever she dashes! That cannot happen, so the two of them are often out of sorts with each other.

■ Intensity Level

Sarah at age twelve is so calm her friends tell her even a tornado would not alarm her. Her younger sister, Susan, on the other hand, becomes excited when a slight breeze blows. Susan reacts to her strict teacher with rage while Sarah is hardly ruffled when a teacher is openly critical of her. The two girls can hardly stand each other. Susan accuses Sarah of overdosing on tranquilizers, and Sarah is sure her sister must have been taking speed. Of course, neither girl is on drugs; they were born very different. Their mother, more like calm Sarah, has problems with both girls. She admires the energy Susan exudes and often wishes she could be more like her. In Sarah, she sees the lack of energy and excitement she dislikes in herself.

■ Predictability

Once you get to know J. B., you can be absolutely certain what to expect. In times of crisis, he will rise to the occasion. You can count on him to have cash, and he will be glad to lend you some. He's uniformly kind and sensitive to a fault to others' feelings. He has a schedule for each day that rarely varies, and you can find him anytime if you know the time of the week. J. B. is highly predictable. That quality is reversed in his father. No one knows what mood he will demonstrate or where he will be on Saturday afternoons. He hates to be held to family schedules, and he would rather eat cold food alone than get home at a regular time. It almost sounds like role reversal, but it is an inborn difference in temperaments. Although each may change some and can certainly develop better balances in habits, the two will always be different.

■ Persistence

For some people, being persistent seems beyond their abilities. They prefer giving up and quitting when they reach demanding spots in a task. They choose jobs that focus on short-term goals and projects that are quick and easy if they are to complete them at all. These people may find it easier to avoid power struggles. They give in all too readily at times. They need help if they are to avoid giving in to peer pressure. Teens are in a specially vulnerable spot when they have too little tenacity.

At the other extreme are strong-willed or downright stubborn persons. On the one hand, they will stick with a project once they start it, but on the other hand, they can annoy parents to no end! When Mom has to run an errand and wants to leave her son off at basketball practice a bit early, she may as well forget it. If he is working on his math homework, he will have to finish it. You can see the potential good in this quality of high persistence but also the problems created in a family in which others have a low level of tenacity. Both "will" and "won't" power create the risk for power struggles.

■ Physical Sensory Threshold

Although two children may register identical patterns on an audiogram, each may experience similar sounds very differently. One may ignore the sound while the other is irritated to the point of yelling by the same sound. Perhaps the most common example is that of hearing a fingernail scraping across a chalkboard. Most of us find that grating sound offensive, but a few people may be unruffled by it.

Some parents told me about their six-year-old, who wanted to watch TV cartoons with her younger brother and sister. The sound of the characters' activities, however, so annoyed her that she turned down the sound. The younger children, unable to hear, turned it back up, and inevitably, a fight ensued. The mother blamed the oldest child for being bossy and selfish, but in her case, that was not true. The kind, loving girl could not tolerate the sounds that the others enjoyed. In the same child, only one or two senses may be highly tuned, or all of them may be.

Imagine how you would feel in an inner-city home. Flashing neon lights, loud, raucous noises day and night, and a lack of secure feelings most of the time are normal for many geographic areas. A supersensitive person experiences daily events with something like that big-city intensity.

One of the explanations for a difficult child's reactions is related to his physical type of sensory vulnerability to ordinary stimulation. When a supersensitive person lives with family members who feel none of the responses he experiences constantly, the person feels lonely and misunderstood.

∎ Withdrawing vs Approach

When I was a little girl, I recall many guests in my home who wanted me to sit on their laps and talk with them. I almost never wanted to do that, yet I did not want to make them feel badly. It was a frustrating predicament. I would look at my dad's face to see if he thought I should go to that person. He would seem to indicate that I should, but he was quick to rescue me. The child who is not comfortable with new situations or unfamiliar people has a high withdrawing quality in her temperament. Children who are less cautious will bravely (or brashly) enter any situation with little or no concern.

In our rather frightening world, the withdrawn child is safer. Caution is most important. It is when either quality becomes extreme that the person is in trouble. The one who withdraws too much will often feel lonely or be seen by others as snobbish. The one who never knows a stranger puts himself at grave risk.

The major stress on the child, however, is not from the outside world but from her family. Arlene was always identified by her siblings and parents as a shy, even fragile child. In time she came to feel different, and she became the scapegoat in her family. Over the years, her withdrawing became so severe that she experienced cycles when she would not leave her house. She finally had a conversation with one sister who expressed genuine concern for her. The simple gesture tipped the scales in a positive direction. She used every bit of her courage and will to reenter normal life events. Some people haven't a sister to care, and many of them grow more and more withdrawn and lonely.

On a day-to-day basis, the outgoing child may have an easier time. People respond to a friendly person in more positive ways than to a shy one. But the danger of overly assertive behaviors is clear.

Eileen is such a child. She wants desperately to be popular, but she tries too hard. Her persistence and intense emotions often make her seem to be bossy. Classmates who start to be friendly with her quickly drift away. She is becoming a child without friends, sad and lonely.

Even with adults, Eileen is an overly assertive, pushy child. Her parents' friends refuse to go out with them when their daughter comes along because they can have no continued conversations with her repeated interruptions. Her inborn tenacity is partly responsible for her inability to change the offensive habits.

Finally, on whichever end of the spectrum a person may be, the difference between child and parent may feed the difficulty. A mother who is outgoing and friendly may try too hard to change a withdrawn child, and ongoing conflicts ensue. Such resentment can build that the two are estranged for life. And yet the answer lies in understanding. The child was born with a different set of temperamental qualities from hers. If the mother can learn to accept the child with his unique, individual characteristics, things will go well. (More of the answers appear in the next chapter.)

■ Adaptability

All children and many adults tend to resist change. As a teenager, I had little patience with my mother's unwillingness to try new recipes or furniture arrangements. She was content with things as they were, and she adamantly refused to change very much. And now I understand her better! As an older person, I no longer like the regular rearrangements in my local grocery store. In fact, I get downright angry when I run in for my urgently needed laundry detergent to find it has been replaced by a shelf of cookies! So I do understand that some children are born resisting change with every fiber of their beings.

The process of being born is a drastic change for a newborn. Leaving the almost total sameness of the environment of the mother's womb for the shockingly different outside world is the most dramatic set of changes most of us ever will experience. As a pediatrician, I always welcomed that cry of indignation of the newborn. It meant the tiny infant had accomplished successfully his first step in the transition we call birth. Some babies cried loud and long, with intense physical reactions. Others cried only a little bit, gently almost, and then fell asleep. Each infant expressed his temperament in the initial cry.

That inborn factor continues throughout life. With more or less change in time, the child grows to adulthood having an easier or more difficult time adapting.

The child who has the hardest time is the one who raises a ruckus when her feeding schedule gets out of order. Later she refuses to stop her play to accommodate

Mom's need to go to the store and take her along. She has an incredibly tough time adjusting to a new teacher, a family move, or the loss of a friend. Making the transition to adolescence is a huge challenge, and leaving home for independence is next to impossible—unless, of course, there is so much controversy she can't wait to leave!

A highly adaptable child can become the too good child you read about earlier in this book. On the other hand, his capacity to accept changes can enable him to sail through life on an even keel.

The poorly adaptive child can sorely try the patience of parents. The youngster resists, in some degree, every change. Even new clothes or toys may be unacceptable to this truly difficult child.

The strong-willed child is familiar to most families. It is my opinion that many of them are children born with poor adaptability. As the equally strong-willed, poorly adaptive parent struggles to *make* the changes happen, conflict between parent and child becomes a way of life. Changes will come, and every child must learn to get along in some degree with those differences.

■ Mood

Newborn babies are a delight to study and evaluate. Some of them are placid; others are intense with energy. Some take great effort to stimulate enough to create a response, and others react wildly to minimal sounds, light, or touch. Some tiny infants have a little frown on their faces, making them appear to be deep in thought. It is by these very early expressions that studies, carried on over time, have shown babies are born with tendencies to certain moods. The mood may be sunny, serious, anxious, or grouchy. The environment can aggravate or relax a child, but the basic response is born with a child.

Let me remind you: it is futile to try to change the inborn qualities of a child's temperament. The best you can do is to understand them, accept them, and gently help your child weave them into the unique, wonderful person she can become.

Even the most difficult temperament reflects a valuable set of qualities. The challenge is to see the potential healthy and unhealthy aspects of each one. Work toward increasing the healthy ones and minimizing the unhealthy ones, and your child will be okay.

Now let's take a look at some of the ways you can help your child grow into a healthy adult.

■─────────────────────────────────

IS IT GENETIC?

Parents of a difficult child are often desperate for help and understanding. The mental health professionals themselves are often at odds about the cause as well as the treatment of these difficulties. There is as yet no foolproof test that can prove if your child needs medication, behavior modification, or more strict disciplinary action.

Controversy continues among various branches of the mental health field about genetic versus environmental factors in emotional problems. Psychiatrists are quick to assert that the problems are all physical, and medication will alleviate them. The studies of Dr. Stella Chess identifying the inborn qualities of temperament would seem to validate that belief.

Other therapists, however, see their clients improve without medication. Through behavioral changes and a different approach within the family, difficult children improve dramatically. Some counselors believe only changes in conduct are required to solve the problems. Others insist that it takes a great amount of thinking and insight to effect the needed changes.

And so it goes—the medicators, the behavioral changers, and the cognitive therapists all believe they are right.

After much study, thinking, and experience, I have found myself in the middle. I can't deny the well-defined studies that show the physical and biochemical changes our clients often experience with medication. Nor can I deny the successes of many therapists whose clients have never taken medication. Many children seem to outgrow their difficult stage, and some of them become outstanding successes.

So somewhere in the middle is the way it is for your child.

I believe this theory fits most difficult children. Genetic factors contribute to the relative ease or difficulty of training and discipline of children. The endocrinological and neurological systems especially affect the temperament of children. No one would deny that these physical systems are inherited just as the color of the eyes, hair, and skin is genetically determined.

The next level of influence comes from the child's immediate family. Members of the extended family enter into this level by either reinforcing the belief that Tim looks so much like Uncle Clayton (who was such a renegade!) or seeing no resemblance at all.

Obviously, the more difficult relatives the child has, the more likely it is that he will run the risk of triggering negative feelings and reactions against him. If a parent has low self-esteem and sees her undesirable traits in her child, she almost certainly will struggle with unconditional acceptance of the child.

A child often experiences the pressure of parental disapproval as rejection. The fear of emotional abandonment results either in rebellion or in excessive attempts to gain a parent's approval. When that sense of pride and pleasure from a parent is missing or in short supply, the child's problem grows. It doesn't matter too much what the problem is; the underlying dynamic is the vital factor.

Now let's add the conflict of mother and child over the elements in their temperaments. When too many of these nine traits oppose each other, there will certainly be trouble, especially in regard to constant attempts to change a child's basic personality. Since these personality traits are inborn, the child cannot change them, and the parent interprets this failure as rebellion. Such overt or even subtle pressures result in an even more intense sense of rejection and fear of abandonment. The parent feels this dynamic just as the child does.

These considerations add up like this:

Genetic factors
+ Family interpretations of them
+ Parent's feelings for and treatment of the child
+ Child's interpretation of parent's reactions
Stress

This combination of factors—and their sum, *stress*—helps create a difficult child of any type. The specific type of difficult child depends on an unpredictable set of accidents, events, and these temperamental factors.

The child's internal stressors and responses to them, added to the external stressors from people close to him, impinging upon the physical characteristics, total stress. The stress in turn stimulates a child's neurological and endocrinological systems to produce more bodily changes.

No one factor in isolation creates a difficult child. It takes some of all these influences to do that. In some, one factor is more powerful; in others, a different problem is dominant. You need to understand all of them if you are to guide your problem child to healthy behaviors.

18

How to Ease
the Difficulty

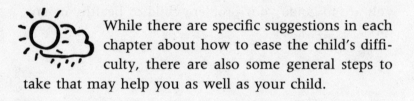 While there are specific suggestions in each chapter about how to ease the child's diffi- culty, there are also some general steps to take that may help you as well as your child.

■
UNCONDITIONAL ACCEPTANCE

For many years, I have known about and taught the essential need for unconditional acceptance. It is more recently that I have understood how that need fits with the inborn qualities of each child's personal tem- perament.

A good parent's job description includes the challenge of identifying and cultivating the child's abilities. The wise parent helps mold each temperamental trait into the best facet of the child it can possibly be. Such shaping through wise and loving discipline and training is a huge, but necessary, task.

The problem is that many parents can't distinguish between changing who the child *is* and correcting how the child *acts*! No one has ever been able to remove my freckles. No one can change my basic adaptability or tendency to withdraw. I have, however, learned to modify my daydreaming, low-activity temperament into a fairly well-disciplined, hardworking lifestyle.

Trying to change the person a child was born to be is not only frustrating but futile. However, recognizing the priceless good in every characteristic with which he is endowed is exciting. Discovering how to shape the traits into a masterpiece is possible.

SEEING THE GOOD

In his immensely insightful book *The Difficult Child,* Dr. Stanley Turecki lists the negative sides of the nine temperamental qualities. Let's see how each one could become valuable as the child grows.

■ High Activity Level

Most parents see a child who is full of energy as a problem. They try to restrict or box in the child. Yet this boundless energy, when harnessed, can enable a teen to become a winner in sports.

■ Highly Distractible

A difficult child forgets responsibilities, daydreams, and can't pay attention. The child can become the fun person in a family. When that daydreamer comes up with her own ideas, she can do some immensely creative things. She needs some correcting, and she may have to learn to write lists, but her basic personality is okay!

■ High-Intensity Level

This trait is quite annoying in childhood, but later it can be an asset. You never need to guess what a high-intensity person is feeling or thinking. He is all too eager to express himself.

■ Highly Unpredictable

This quality can try the patience of parents of younger children. By adolescence, with good training, this trait can introduce a level of spontaneity that adds great spice to family living.

■ Negative Persistence

Trying to pry your son away from his construction set so you can get to the drugstore before it closes is a challenge. But look ahead. If you train him right, that very quality can enable him to say no to drug use or other destructive behaviors.

■ Low Sensory Threshold

A supersensitive child affects the lifestyle of the entire family. This quality, however, can enable your adult child to be discriminating with a constructive critical-ness that can create a peaceful environment. Constructive criticism finds out what's wrong so it can be righted. It also finds out what's good so it can be commended.

■ Initial Withdrawal

People may not know how to react to your shy or snob-bish-appearing child. But seeing your child secure from potentially harmful strangers can make you rejoice. How will you perceive it?

■ Poor Adaptability

Even the loveliest new clothes are unacceptable to a child who can't adapt. She'd prefer to wear old faded clothes than stylish new ones. This can be a great disappointment to a mom who takes pride in the way her child looks. If Mom can look beyond the present (in this case, the present may extend well into adolescence), she will see this quality can be trained into good study and work habits. Sticking tenaciously with a task until it's well done is a fine quality.

■ Negative Mood

Once this unpleasant trait is balanced, the child who owns it can become less grouchy and will become a serious person. Steering her away from the extremes of worry, anxiety, and anger can enable this trait to help its owner become a conscientious person.

I'll admit, I had to stretch some of these unpleasant traits quite a bit to come up with some positives. I suspect you can do much better. I trust that you get the point. Find a way to turn irritating qualities in your child in a positive direction. Even attempting to see the good will change your attitude. I can almost guarantee that your child's mood will follow yours.

◼
APPROVAL

W hile acceptance must be unconditional, approval is, by definition, conditional. Pride in baby's first steps means he has to risk standing upright and moving his feet. Pride in her good school papers means she puts effort into learning. And pride in your adolescent's drug- and sex-free lifestyle really means he has accomplished healthy independence and wise decision making.

The trouble with parenting difficult kids is that it demands so much effort to get them to do anything that everyone is exhausted and angry at the end. I assigned to Julie and her mother the task of getting her room cleaned and orderly before I saw them the next week. Sixteen-year-old Julie was extremely stubborn, and she was comfortable with her disaster-stricken room. Both agreed they would accomplish the task, and I eagerly awaited their next appointment.

Both of them appeared glum, and I was afraid they

had failed in the assignment. They had, in fact, accomplished the job by midnight prior to their visit. Mom nagged; Julie resisted; both became angry and miffed. Frustrated Mom admitted, however, that it was at least a decent job.

As I watched anger, guilt, and sadness flit across Julie's face, I realized that she needed solace, not another scolding. So I turned my attention to Mom. "Did you," I asked, "remember to thank Julie for her efforts?"

Mom literally exploded! "What do you mean, did I thank her? She should thank me! If I hadn't made her do it, that job would never have been done!"

I could certainly understand the mother's frustration. Yet I knew she needed to acknowledge that Julie did two heroically difficult tasks: she cleaned her room, and she bent her will to that of her mother. I explained that for doing both jobs, Julie deserved appreciation.

I learned only as a grandmother that the harder it is for a child to bend his will, even though the attitude may leave something to be desired, the more credit he deserves.

As a mother, I'm afraid I was too busy to discover the perspective that taking time affords. I hope you parents will try to slow down and take a good look at the whole of the situations you must face from day to day.

In every situation, even those in which there are more problems than achievements, you must look for a positive, redemptive element. It takes that attitude to keep hope alive in a youngster's heart and maintain the parent-child bond. As long as your child knows you love her and you offer hope for the future, together you can cope with anything.

■

POLISHING DIAMONDS

Whatever values you may believe in and practice will help establish the loving relationship that best motivates your child. At the age of fifteen, I had to live away from home in a small apartment with my sister in order to complete high school during the war. The arrangement was necessary since gasoline was rationed and driving from our farm home to high school was impossible. I cannot imagine allowing my children to leave home at such a tender age. But my parents could do it for these reasons:

- They trusted God to look after us.
- They trusted their own sound parenting.
- They valued a good education.
- They knew we loved them so much that we would never have done anything to disappoint them.

We wouldn't have, and we didn't. We had our share of sibling rivalry and competition, but we handled our lives remarkably well. We kept our rooms clean, fixed nutritious meals, and responsibly managed our finances. Our parents had carefully been polishing their rough diamonds, and they knew we would be okay, so we never doubted that.

I have explained that you cannot change your child's basic temperament or personality. But you can polish the rough edges to bring out the loveliness of your jewel. And that polishing process is what training and discipline are about.

Here are some rules for training your child:

- Have a logical set of goals and plans. Don't impulsively react to your child.
- Take time to really understand your child. Review the nine qualities of temperament, and decide if your child registers high or low on them. See which *one* needs balancing most.
- Never punish your child for who she is, but consistently correct the wrongs she does.
- Use the least severe consequence that will teach the needed lesson.
- Always offer hope and forgiveness.
- Avoid long lectures, but be sure your child understands the rule, the consequence, and the basic lesson he should learn.
- Follow through consistently, lovingly, and firmly. The best lessons are packaged in love!

FORGIVENESS AND RECONCILIATION

Peggy was naturally happy and often mischievous. Only rarely was she malicious, but whenever she did something quite wrong, her father would punish her plenty! He administered a lecture, gave her a ceremonious spanking, and then ignored her for days. She never knew when he might return to being a reasonably kind parent.

From Peggy's earliest memories through her adolescence, her father never wavered in his corrective actions. She endured them and tried to honor her austere dad. By far the most painful part of the punishment was his emotional coldness. She panicked even as she described the total abandonment and hopelessness she felt during those long days of his withdrawal. At no time could she recall any sense of forgiveness, and a widening chasm split their relationship.

Forgiveness is grossly misunderstood. On the one extreme, people pass it off as a glib statement that they mean only superficially and fail to really understand. On the other extreme are popular counselors who say that forgiveness is wrong because it absolves the offender of responsibility. Let's explore in some depth how to achieve forgiveness that is complete. This plan does not absolve the offender, but it prevents bitterness in the victim.

The dictionary, religious teachings, and my own experience see forgiveness differently. *Webster's New World Dictionary* says *to forgive* is "to give up resentment against, or the desire to punish; stop being angry with; pardon; to give up all claim to punish or exact penalty for."

The truth is that forgiveness works! It frees the victim from bitterness and prevents the retaliation that can keep in motion a cycle of wounding each other. It offers the offender hope for a new beginning and the prospect of doing better. It may even motivate the offender to apologize and make restitution, though these actions do not always follow.

If you have a difficult child, you must understand the problem is his and it is not aimed at you. Don't take the difficult child's behavior to heart. Do help your child recognize the hurt in his wrongdoing, and do help him correct it. With a young child you may *require* correction. Sometimes an adolescent, with time and guidance, will own misdeeds and make amends.

Here are the steps to complete forgiveness. They are *so* worth taking!

■ Acknowledge Your Pain

Pride often makes people deny that anyone can hurt them. You can prevent others from destroying you, but anytime you love another person, you give the person some power to hurt you.

■ Discover Why She Inflicted Pain

Perhaps you hurt her first and didn't know it. Maybe you misinterpreted what she said or did. Possibly, whatever she did reminded you of events from your past. Usually, there are some explanations that will help you understand why your offender hurt you.

■ Choose to Allow the Information to Become Understanding

This step requires that you have a heart open to forgiveness as well as a collection of information to use. It is most tempting to hang on to old hurts and the anger they create. But over time, yielding to that temptation will allow bitterness to grow beyond your control. You see, in the long run, forgiveness makes you a better person even more than it helps your offender.

■ Let It Go

When all the pain is acknowledged, the information is gathered, and the insight is complete, you must decide to let go of the hurtful event. Whether that is a huge offense or a small misunderstanding, the eventual relinquishment is essential. Bringing up past problems only adds to a child's difficulty. You must make a conscious decision to take this step, and you will probably have to repeat the step several times. But following through will complete the process of forgiveness and reconciliation.

You can ease the difficulty that's affecting your child. You may need help from friends, family, and a professional counselor. But living with pain is certain to cause problems in your entire family. So do your best to guide your child to healthy ways of living.

19
The Importance of a Father

Bernard's teenage masculinity was about to crumble as we talked. He was moderately good-looking and not very muscular, but he tried hard to be manly. He wanted to be a sports hero, and he worked out faithfully so he could possibly make the football team. Every day he practiced, however, he felt more defeated. He wasn't as good as the other guys. If only he had an older brother! He'd given up long ago expecting help from his dad. He was gone a lot, was too tired a lot and, Bernard suspected, didn't care a lot. The approval and pride the young man craved from Dad were not there.

By contrast, the presence of my father, even in memory, was a central security of my entire life. He seemed to crave my being with him as a child, and I always felt that I was important to him. He shared with me stories of his childhood, discoveries in nature, and stimulating ideas from his reading and profound thinking. He taught me, almost incidentally, how to think and in some degree to make sense out of the knowledge I had. My father's gift of humor was balanced by his unusual sensitivity and the ability to take seriously those issues that warranted concern. His physical strength was immense, and I always knew that with him I was safe.

Paul had a missing father. While Bernard's dad was missing in his role as a father, Paul's dad had literally abandoned him and his mother and brother. Repeatedly, he would call and set up fun things to do with his son, but he rarely followed through. If he did, he was so late, Paul's worry and frustration spoiled the fun he had counted on.

Three fathers, all common in today's culture. Yes, there are many wonderful dads—men who love their kids and put them ahead of their interests and needs. Then there are the dads who express their love by making a living for their families. They often do not know how to interact with their children and are even uncomfortable with their wives. And finally, there are all too many fathers who abandon their children more or less completely.

It has been my experience that the delinquent dads don't like letting down their children. They want to be good fathers, but they do not know how, or their severe personal problems prevent them from providing the needed help.

For so many years, it has been accepted that fathers are dispensable. They are occasionally brought to court for failure to pay child support, but there is little pressure, if any at all, to get them to pay attention to their children. No one requires them to take a child fishing or attend a child's recital.

Over the years, I have worked with thousands of troubled children and teenagers. In the majority of their histories is a common denominator: Dad wasn't there. From being in prison to being too busy, the absent father was the source of major grief for most of the kids. Whether their dads abused them or neglected them, the young people were damaged.

Let me hasten to state that by no means is every troubled youth plagued with a terrible father. Some of the dads tried the best they knew to be good parents. But all too commonly, there was more difficulty related to dads.

A GOOD FATHER

In my book *Mothering*, I reviewed the studies of Dr. Harry Harlow at the University of Wisconsin. He discovered the damage that occurred when baby monkeys were removed from their mothers at birth. As the babies matured, they evidenced major problems in conceiving infant monkeys, and those who did so had no idea about caring for their young. Although humans are not comparable to monkeys, the truth is clear. No matter what the species, mothers' loving care of their young imprints in them the substance of passing on good care.

To my knowledge, no one has done any similar studies of fathers. Yet *Cruden's Concordance*, which lists every word in the Bible, has six complete columns of references to fathers—in fine print. Evidently, dads are important.

Occasionally, family researchers state that fathers are highly influential forces in children's lives. The support by two parents of each other provides the healthy matrix in which children can mature with less difficulty.

William, at age fourteen, was a sturdy eighth grader. Bright and well-liked by his peers, he refused to attend school. At the time, I was a pediatrician, and I still made house calls. William's mother called me in desperation, asking me to stop by and see if together we could budge him out of his room and onto the school bus.

When I saw William, he was slumped over his desk in his nicely appointed room. With eyes downcast and voice muffled, he finally talked with me. "All I need," he informed me, "is my dad to pry me loose!" Then his grief poured out. His parents didn't get along well. After sixteen years of an unhappy marriage, Dad walked out. William loved his dad, though he tested his authority to the limit. He found it easy to defy his permissive mother, and he knew exactly what was missing—Dad's strength! It took weeks to help William heal from the grief of his loss, and the scars remain today. William left his own imperfect marriage, and his sons suffered a loss much like his own a generation ago.

In the Bible, there are these sobering words: "The Lord is longsuffering and abundant in mercy, forgiving iniquity and transgression; but He by no means clears the guilty, visiting the iniquity of the fathers on the children to the third and fourth generation" (Num. 14:18).

It seems to me that God intended fathers to imprint good in the lives of their children. Then mercy will be shown "to thousands, to those who love Me [God] and keep My commandments" (Exod. 20:6).

As you consider the contrast between William's father and mine, you can understand these Scriptures. Dr. Harlow and others are discovering some ways in which the ancient knowledge is lived out.

A father's unique strength in a family offers protection and permission. They may lead to good or ill, but the influence is powerful. Let's consider some qualities of a good father.

■ A Good Father Values His Child

The child is important to him—enough that he sacrifices his pleasures to find time to spend with the child. He will avoid wasting money to be able to supply the child's material needs.

■ A Good Father Provides for His Child

The traditional head of a family sees to it that the child's needs are met and then takes care of his own need. The needs are for living acceptance, meaningful discipline and training, and building character.

■ A Good Father Shows Compassion for His Child

A beautiful psalm states, "As a father pities his children, so the Lord pities those who fear Him" (Ps. 103:13).

Pity can be a quality that puts down its object. That is not what a good dad does. When I was eight years old, my father took me and my sister to hear a concert played by the U.S. Marine band. Our town was small, and music of that caliber was rarely available. At some sacrifice, we attended to find only standing room at the very rear of the long auditorium. I was entranced by the exquisite music, but I could see none of the natty uniforms or the brilliance of their polished brass instruments. My compassionate father took pity on me. He lifted me onto his shoulders where to my utter delight, I could view the whole scene. That was the pity of a good father.

It is right for a child to do independently everything possible. That's the way she becomes responsible and mature. But when there is something a child wants and needs ever so much to do, but she just can't do it, the pity of a good father helps her out.

■ A Good Father Leads or Guides His Child

A comforting statement is found in this psalm:

> I will instruct you and teach you
> in the way which you should go;
> I will guide you with My eye (Ps. 32:8).

My father had the most expressive brown eyes! A mere glance at them told me if he was teasing, if it was a serious-but-not-threatening situation, or if it was a no-nonsense urgent situation. He could look at any of his seven children, and without a word, we usually knew what he expected of us. At no time was I afraid of him. I knew he had my best interests at heart. I allowed my dad to guide me with his eye, so I can understand a tiny bit about the heavenly Father.

Good dads guide their kids by their example, their words, and their beliefs and priorities. Much of this guidance takes place on a nonverbal level, yet it is powerful.

■ A Good Father Protects His Child

From memories of my earliest years, I can recall countless ways in which my father protected me. One of the most vivid was a bitterly cold day in January. On the flatlands of central Kansas, there was little to break the driving force of the north winds.

On that especially cold day, not one farm vehicle would start. It was unthinkable that my sister and I should miss school, so our parents bundled us up in all the layers of warm clothing we could get on. As we left the house to walk into that cold gusty wind, Dad called us back. He feared our noses could be frostbitten, so he wrapped up in his warmest coats to go with us.

My father had nearly died some time earlier from pneumonia, and in those days, folks believed one caught pneumonia from being too cold. Nevertheless, Dad walked before us, hoping his sturdy frame would break the force of the wind. He realized that even his body could not protect the two of us. He courageously unbuttoned his overcoat, holding it open to shield us. In doing so, he believed he might suffer, but he loved us so much, he took that risk.

Few fathers today need to risk their health and their very lives as my father did. But there are far worse dangers that threaten the moral fiber, the very souls, of their children. Fathers need to monitor the TV programs their children watch, the books they read, and the concepts they are taught.

Just as my father could not stop the north wind, dads today cannot stem the tide of violence, false values, and obsessive interest in material goods. It is too great at this time. But they can think and they can teach their offspring to think. They can help kids understand what makes anything right or wrong. They can teach clear judgment of good and bad, and they can teach the self-control and willpower that will enable their children to choose wisely.

■ A Good Father Sticks with His Child

William knew exactly what he needed—his dad's strength to get him to school. A good dad doesn't abandon his child. He works hard at building a healthy marriage to provide the intact family boundaries a child needs. If, in the rare instance, maintaining the marriage is impossible, he still sticks with the child. He may need to sacrifice job promotions or career opportunities. But what a small price to pay for assuring a healthy child! He may even give up his favorite hobby or TV programs if they rob his child of too much of himself. Dad's presence, encouraging, correcting, or challenging his child, is irreplaceable.

■ A Good Father Relinquishes His Child

As a child develops, the boundaries must expand. A wise dad knows the child's sense of responsibility and just how much freedom the child can handle. By gradually expanding the limits, he can teach the child to adjust to broader horizons. Allowing too much freedom too early or too little too late will set the scene for rebellion.

My father knew my sister and I were ready for the amazing amount of responsibility we assumed as teens. Living quite on our own, we knew that we could make it. And so we did. His confidence in us challenged us to live up to the best standards possible.

The poignant story of the prodigal son in Luke 15:11–32 tells the risk of letting go of a child. The wise father of a foolish son gave him his share of his inheritance and watched him leave home. I suspect the father knew his son would soon waste his entire fortune. Yet the father allowed him to do so. He sent no emissaries to bring him home. In fact with that tough love, only known in the wisest parent, he waited until his son hit absolute bottom. And the father watched. He must have looked down that dusty road countless times because he saw his son in the distance when he finally returned home. His son could learn only from experience, and the father trusted their love to draw him back when the lessons were mastered.

Letting go of even the least difficult child involves risk and is a wrenching experience. But only when the separation of father and child is complete can the child become an adult and create the next generation. When a child is as impulsive and rebellious as the son in this Scripture, relinquishment may be torture. But in the long run, it may be the only way to save the child.

■ A Good Father Is a Safe Harbor for Returning in Later Storms

Though I am three times a grandmother and my father has been dead some thirty years, he still is a place for me to retreat. Whenever I can, I drive to the picturesque country church across the road from my childhood home. The house and barn are long gone, though I treasure mementos from them.

But the memories of my father's life and guidance, his wisdom and protection, his integrity and constancy, are all there. I see him patting his old horse and walking with his collie, always wanting to give me some gift from his garden or cellar whenever I visited. He is a place, a person, to whom I can return, even in memory, for a refresher course in being a real person!

You see, fathers are important. They can make the difference in keeping a child from becoming a difficult one. I hope you dads will face your challenge with courage and persevere in your task!

20

Faith in Power Beyond Your Own

There are so many voices shrieking philosophies about families. They advocate strictness, lenience, openness, and structure. What are you to believe, and how can you know what is *the* truth?

In my nearly seven decades of life, I have listened to countless hours of lectures, read stacks of books, and even written a few. While there is vast knowledge in my world, I consistently turn for ultimate truth to the Bible, that age-old collection of God's wisdom. It is remarkably concise and certainly correct.

It has stood through time, it makes sense, and more often than not, scientific discoveries validate its truth.

In this chapter, I will share with you some of the spiritual aspects of coping with a difficult child and preventing the conditions in many cases that may cause a child to become a problem.

IS THE ROD REALLY NECESSARY?

The advocates of harsh punishment have taken as their authority statements from the book of Proverbs:

> Foolishness is bound up in the heart of a child;
> The rod of correction will drive it far from him
> (22:15).

> He who spares his rod hates his son,
> But he who loves him disciplines him promptly
> (13:24).

> Chasten your son while there is hope,
> And do not set your heart on his destruction
> (19:18).

Believe me, I struggled valiantly over these gems of God's wisdom—a gift to King Solomon at his request. They have been interpreted commonly as a reason to physically chastise children.

In my daily work, however, I had to face the facts of the growing menace of child abuse. I understand the amount of stress affecting parents, and I know how quickly their anger outstrips their control and their reason.

I have searched, prayed, and pondered about the use of the rod. And these ideas are the result of my efforts. We must understand the rod.

As a girl, I had the pleasant duty of watching our sheep. That experience reminded me of perhaps the most well-known portion of Scripture, the Shepherd's Psalm:

> I will fear no evil;
> For You are with me;
> Your rod and Your staff, they comfort me
> (Ps. 23:4).

The parallel of the good shepherd and the good parent is superb!

A good parent is always observing the child, watching out for the tendency to stray too near danger. Rather than angrily striking him, a wise parent will nudge him back on track. If he gets too far out of safety, the parent will lift him up and put him back where he belongs.

The rod is necessary. But it dare not be a rod of rage. Instead, it is the symbolic rod of wise protective authority, used to prevent a child's straying into danger. A New Testament writer offered this advice: "And you, fathers, do not provoke your children to wrath, but bring them up in the training and admonition of the Lord" (Eph. 6:4).

Anger generates anger. Whipping a child out of the parent's rage will almost certainly cause rebellion with its destructive retaliation. Our news media consistently report the tragic drama of children murdering parents. You can count on it: most of those events were the end result of angry parenting.

You can get by with punishment by intimidation only as long as you are stronger than your child. When she outgrows you, you must look out!

RELYING ON GOD'S RESOURCES

The Bible is a reliable guide in child rearing, and if all concepts are kept in perspective, you are very likely to raise a child who is not difficult. Not only is the Bible an accurate guidebook for parenting, it also teaches the source for parents' energy and wisdom:

> The fear of the LORD is the
>   beginning of wisdom,
> And the knowledge of the Holy
>   One is understanding (Prov. 9:10).

The vast wisdom of the Bible is available for your mastery. Story after story illustrates that God uses ordinary people in extraordinary ways when they trust Him and follow His ways. When they ignore God and choose to rely only on themselves, they predictably end up in trouble.

In few areas of life does such a philosophy cause such great disaster as in family living. Relying only on your own resources can result in serious pain! But you need not do that. Discovering God's power—and adopting it as your own—is an active process.

My experience has shown me God's resources are available to me, but He does not shower them on me. I must take an active part in finding and learning how to use them.

First, you need to know God so that you are aware of the qualities He offers you, the example He has set, and the ways that knowledge can affect your parenting methods. Reading the Bible will teach you about these basic ways of living.

Knowing God will enable you to find the grace and strength to make peace with others and yourself. God will enable you to understand the difficult people around you and the painful personality problems that invade your being.

One of the wonderful aspects of knowing God is that it enables me to practice communication better. I try to imagine God being with me. I can and do pray to God in heaven, but I often need the presence of God near me. He knows our dilemmas and the frailties from which we must operate.

Some people talk about God speaking to them. I really don't know if they hear an audible voice, but I never have. What does occur is the great sense of His love, and in my mind, I experience wise thoughts. Sometimes they come in memories reassuring me of God's power in past perils. At times they appear with a touch of humor as ideas I could try. Sometimes the thoughts offer insight or understanding about a person or situation.

You can see how deeply these ideas penetrate into the ways you parent. It's easier to allow hurts and misunderstandings to collect than to deal with them a day at a time. But the accumulations become huge barriers estranging you from your child. The apostle Paul wrote, " 'Be angry, and do not sin': do not let the sun go down on your wrath" (Eph. 4:26). I practice this every day, absolutely refusing to let resentment or hurt become anger or bitterness.

Living with God is never easy, I've discovered, but it is an exciting adventure in finding peace, love, and joy.

■

THE DECISION TO LOVE

Love is sadly misunderstood. It is described as a feeling or an accident. People "fall" in love. People who are involved in affairs or who have a "crush" on someone describe their experience as being bigger than they are—overwhelming in magnitude.

It is one thing to fall in love with another adult, but unfortunately, that philosophy has invaded relationships between parents and children! A mother told me that she doesn't like her child. She rationalized that she really loves him but doesn't like him. That arrangement is possible, but in talking with her child, I learned that he does not feel her love, either. The two of them are terribly at odds.

Love, you see, is a decision. It is enlarged by the self-control that enables you to act loving even when you feel out of sorts or downright miserable. It begins with loving God and receiving God's love in turn. It grows with loving yourself, and it is completed in loving others: " 'You shall love the LORD your God with all your heart, with all your soul, with all your strength, and with all your mind,' and 'your neighbor as yourself' " (Luke 10:27).

This love is not defined by feelings alone; it is a total effort of body, mind, emotions, and spirit. Love is often tender, nurturing, and compassionate. It may just as well be stern, brook no nonsense, and set clear limits.

We often call this tough love, and it is just as important as the tender variety.

It takes tough love to protect children, but it does not need to be mean or angry. Practicing tough love seems to me to be godly.

This evening I was reminiscing with a relative about our parenting style of years ago. Both of us grew up with critical, lecturing parents, but each of us tried to avoid copying their methods. She described the way she corrected her boys. "I would get right into their faces, look them in the eye, and tell them seriously what I felt they needed to know," she said. It usually worked for her, and if she ever did have to raise her voice, they really listened.

I experienced my walk with God similarly. He handles people as gently as they will allow. Only when they fail to listen or obey does God speak in sterner tones to them. Because He loves His children so much, He won't let them get by with wrongdoing forever.

■

IN TOUCH WITH GOD

Many people seem to be unable to get in touch with God. And I suspect there is no exact formula for how to really know Him. But this illustration may help if you are searching.

During a particularly baffling period, I disciplined my life to allow for a more regular prayer time than usual. On one occasion I was in a meditative mood and gazed at a spot on the wall in my study. It happened to be the electrical outlet. Nothing about it was at all unusual. It was well-dusted, and it accented the color of the wall.

Near the outlet was a floor lamp. It had been carefully selected to fit into the decor, and it was in perfect working order. The problem was, it was dark. In that unique way I've already described, God placed neatly in my thoughts a profound truth.

The power in my wall was immense, and it was available to the lamp. The lamp was lovely but useless. It was not plugged in. By a voluntary, rather complex set of motions, I bent down, picked up the plug, and inserted it into the power source. With a quick flick of the switch, I turned on the lamp, and it glowed beautifully, lighting up my room.

And that is how it is to relate to God. God made of me a pretty good person. He is the inexhaustible power Source. But He didn't make me a robot whom He could wind up and set in motion. If I'm to know His power— even more important, to know Him—I have some responsibility. I have to choose to plug myself in and turn on my switch. He'll see to it the power flows, accomplishing whatever the Designer chooses.

CHOOSE NOT TO GO IT ALONE

For help in parenting a difficult child or trying to keep your child from becoming difficult, God is there. For wisdom, love, rightness, and energy, God is the supplier. For whatever your need, He cares.

People are amazingly capable of handling life's challenges. They often do so well, in fact, that they convince themselves they really don't need God. Sooner or later, however, they will. And when it comes to raising a healthy child, it seems foolish to risk going it alone. I hope you'll try plugging in if you haven't already!

21

I've Failed! Is There Hope?

With tears dripping down her cheeks, Kelley sat in my office wailing, "I've failed so miserably, Dr. Grace. What can I possibly do to make it up to my child?" Kelley had experienced one of those priceless moments in which she had that flash of insight about her child. It was a moment counselors wait for! He was one of those hard-to-raise kids with a temperament directly opposite hers. She had made every effort to force him to change—with no success—and she came to feel he was against her, deliberately making her life as difficult as possible.

Realizing that she had emotionally rejected her son, leaving him feeling abandoned, had crushed Kelley. She wanted to be a good mother, and she really did love her son. But the marked differences between them had gotten to her over his twelve-year life span. Kelley, I knew, would work as hard as she could to repair the damage to her son and their relationship.

I have sat with friends over morning coffee, patients in my office, and relatives in my living room, sharing their grief over mistakes that resulted in making their children difficult. I have sat alone, grieving over my own mistakes. Some of us make more errors than others, but every parent goofs at some time.

WHAT ARE THE ANSWERS?

The answers, of course, lie in the *awareness of one's mistakes*. Since parents try too hard to be great, they find it easy to rationalize their errors. It must be the sitter, the teachers, the friends, or the child herself. They almost pray, "Please, God, don't let this problem be me!"

But at least part of the problem does lie with you, the parent. This knowledge could cause you to wallow in guilt, but that is not very helpful, except to awaken in you the insight you need. Guilt with its pain can remind you that you must change, and that is the core of hope —changing. The exciting message is that you can be different. The not-so-exciting message is that it takes lots of work.

YOUR CHILD'S ROLE

The next part of the answer lies in taking the time and trouble to really understand your child. Take a look at the nine components of temperament. In which ones is your child on the positive end of the spectrum? Which ones are weak? Are there some clearly negative areas? Let's review them.

1. *Activity level*
- He is calm and placid.
- She is busy and active.
- He is restless and hyperactive.
- She is a wild wall climber.

2. *Distractibility*
- He plays all morning or studies all evening (depending on age).
- She stays with a task for a good length of time (compared with others).
- He has trouble sticking with any job.
- She can't focus at all and forgets quickly what she was assigned to do.

3. *Intensity level*
- He is laid-back and relaxed about most things.
- She gets excited or upset about a few things that matter to her.
- He reacts intensely to most things, positively or negatively.
- No matter what it is, she has a prompt, intense reaction.

4. *Predictability*
- You can set the clock by this child's innate structure.
- Now and then he forgets dinner or insists on staying up later.
- It's hard to know when she'll be grouchy or why she's nicer than usual.

- You never know why he's moody or when it will change.

5. *Persistence*
- She is blithe and cooperative, almost always gives in.
- At times he sticks up for his wishes or decisions.
- She holds out extensively to get her way.
- He gets so tied to having things his way, no one can stand him.

6. *Sensory threshold*
- The loudest thunder never awakens her, and she loves bright lights and colors.
- He is somewhat startled by noises or sudden motion, and he doesn't like many foods.
- She can't stand rough textures and acts nervous when the environment is very stimulating or new.
- He is very upset by most sensory stimuli—light, temperature, noise, taste, activity level, or smell.

7. *Withdrawal vs approach*
- She never knows a stranger; she is outgoing and friendly to a fault.
- He is fairly extroverted but cautious; he prefers time to assess the situation before entering into it.
- She is quite reserved and will interact with others only in her own way and time.
- He refuses to have anything to do with new people —the first day of the school year is panic time.

8. *Adaptability*
- She gets excited over new toys or clothes; moving is a great adventure.

- He likes new things but hangs on to many old, familiar things as well. After a while he can accept a family move.
- She doesn't really like new things and seems to fear they will displace old, familiar ones. She really hates to think of a family move.
- He clings tenaciously to old, familiar things—even dislikes new clothes or games.

9. *Mood*

- A happy, effervescent mood prevails most of the time. She is optimistic.
- He has times when he feels sad or angry, but these are explainable and short in duration.
- More than her peers, she is grouchy and hard to get along with. But at times she bounces into a pleasant, happy mood.
- Most of the time he is unpleasant; he is never effervescent. He usually is pessimistic and lives in shades of gray to black mood.

Almost no child is consistently in the top grade bracket, and few are always at the bottom. As you rate your child, no matter what the age, think back to birth and early childhood. You will almost certainly find those traits you have defined go back to birth. This information can help you let go of any feeling that you may have about your child intentionally making life as difficult as possible for you. They are traits that can keep your child unhappy and negatively affect the formation and maintenance of healthy relationships.

EVALUATE YOURSELF

The third part in redeeming your mistakes lies in assessing your temperament. Now that you have somewhat clearly defined your child's personality, take time to see yourself in those nine categories as well. You might take a retrospective look. How were you as a child? How are you different now? And best of all, can you define how and when you changed (if you have!)? This last question can help you in working with your child.

If you haven't changed as much as you would like to, now is the time to do so. Here are some steps to change:

1. Be honest and aware enough of the need to change that you will be motivated to do the hard work that change demands.
2. Give yourself permission to change. Most of us get stuck in habits for unconscious reasons. Being too different is frightening and makes changing difficult.
3. Make a plan for changing. A client of mine resisted this step for a week, then on a ten-minute break at work she wrote up a superb one. Without a plan, change will at best be erratic.
4. Organize some help. Recruit a few people you can trust to support you in changing. They should range from blunt and critical to encouraging and kind. You'll need both extremes. Above all, include the help of God, whose telephone is never busy!

5. Be persistent. From organizing a plan to achieving success, you will be tempted to quit. The old way won't seem so bad; the effort will feel futile; the journey will look far too rough. Don't believe these fallacies. Just stick with it.

6. Enjoy the results!

Formulating a plan seems to confound many people. Yet each person, I have discovered, needs to work on that individually. However, these examples may help you.

Let's assume that your child is supersensitive to physical stimuli. She can't stand the spicy foods that other family members enjoy. When the TV or radio is too loud, she shrieks at her siblings to turn it down. She often turns out lights, and she can't stand the scent of your favorite perfume.

You have just understood that she was born with this excessive physical sensitivity, but you have chastised her and punished her for years. You now recognize that she can't help her sensitivity, but you know she must learn to modify her reactions. This may be your plan:

- Sit alone with her, and talk about your mistakes and lack of understanding. Tell her you are committed to change.
- Help her understand herself and accept her sensory awareness. Enable her to see how it may bring joy in her life.
- Together try to formulate better patterns for her responses. For example, explain to her brothers how annoying loud sounds are to her. Getting their co-

operation in reducing the sound level to moderation can create a sense of empathy and healthy bonding.

- Ask her what she needs from you to help her modify her behavior, and decide together what you need from her to help you stop chastising her.
- Try keeping a count of the times you succeed and the times you fail. You may expect plenty of failures at first since old habits are powerful and hard to break.
- I recommend a special reward for success. Keep rewards simple and inexpensive, and be sure they're fun for both of you.

DON'T BECOME PERMISSIVE

There is so much danger of becoming a permissive, anything-goes parent, I feel I must warn you! I have already explained in the chapter on rebellion that too much leniency can cause serious difficulty in a child.

If you have been too harsh and have tried to change your child's personality, you are at risk of feeling guilty. Knowing you have tried to make your son be a person he can't may make you feel bad. At first, you will prefer to think this entire concept is dead wrong. That way you can continue to be right, but your child will suffer for your persistence (stubbornness)!

No, I have not joined the ranks of the liberal thinkers or New Age philosophers. I'm staying with the commonsense, practical approach that has always worked. The whole idea is that you stay firm regarding family policies. Everyone must follow them. Some kids will do so more promptly and with a sweeter attitude than others. Stay logical and loving; give encouragement when it's needed and praise when it's deserved. And avoid being abusive. Be patient.

The specific kinds of difficult kids and ways to cope with them are described earlier in the book. In summary, correcting past mistakes demands gaining insight, knowing yourself and your child, and finding that vital balance of firmness and flexibility, approval and disapproval, being consistent and loving throughout. Maintain a sense of humor as a useful asset as long as it is not aimed at anyone's self-worth.

■
DON'T BECOME ABUSIVE

When you reach your breaking point with your difficult child, you may call names, make negative predictions, or hit your child. Such breaking point behaviors need to be handled carefully.

First, be quick to apologize for your methods. Damaging a child's spirit and marring his self-esteem are not in the job description of a healthy parent. Don't do that, and if you ever have, seek your child's forgiveness.

Next, hold on tenaciously to the values and goals you have set for your child in terms of behaviors and attitudes. Just as surely as you *can't* change your child's inborn temperament, you *can* guide her away from erroneous ideas and obnoxious behaviors.

Build as strong a bond of love with your child as you possibly can. Do this by working on yourself so that you honestly feel loving and accepting toward your child. Express this love in words and through affection as often as you think of it. Find all the positives present in your child, and comment on your appreciation and respect for them. If you have a highly sensitive child, express your feelings gently, but keep consistent in doing that.

■ A CYCLE STOPPED

Stella was a truly difficult child. She was expelled from the third grade. She had intimidated her two brothers and two sisters. Even her parents were afraid of her violent temper tantrums. What was bothering Stella? She had perceived that her parents hated her. She had picked up rather foul language, and they found themselves labeling her a tyrant, an impossible child, and even worse. The family had developed a vicious circle of emotional abuse.

An aggressive child creating havoc in her family, Stella had taken over destructive control of her entire family. Fortunately, her mother realized how estranged she and her daughter had become. She really did love Stella and was willing to seek help. She began to hug her child. Instead of banishing Stella from the kitchen, her mother was able to state convincingly, "Stella, it's so neat that you want to be near me. Welcome to our kitchen. Want to help make toast?"

It took time, but once again, love and wisdom prevailed. Stella basked in her mother's renewed expressions of love and began to love her back. Bit by little bit, Stella became less difficult. She actually became a family

star—evidence of concerted efforts to stop negative behaviors. The damage of temperamental conflicts, their
misinterpretation, and the vicious circle that develops
out of that mixture of factors takes a toll in families like
Stella's. But they can also know a whole new way of
living.

■

THE DIFFICULT PARENT

Throughout this book, I have had to write about
the mistakes of parents. All too often these errors are serious enough to result in harm to their children. And my experience has proved to me that parents not only do not intend to hurt their children but
also are filled with remorse when they discover that
they have.

If you are one of those parents, honest enough to see
and admit your mistakes, what can you do to make
amends? How can you prevent the possibility of grave
estrangement from your child after he is grown?

Several of my older friends have adult children who
have recalled painful abuse from the parents in their
early years. They have become so angry and unforgiving
that they cut off all relationships with their parents.
They will not even allow their children to see their
grandparents.

From what I have already written about forgiving,
you know how needless such bitterness is. Furthermore,
new studies are raising questions about the validity of
these retrieved memories. There are realistic possibilities
that some of them are suggested by overzealous counsel-

ors. While I agree that this is true, I know with equal confidence that real abuse has often occurred.

It is so crucial to prevent estrangement and promote the healing of any hurts you may have inflicted on your child. No matter how right your motives, your methods were wrong if they left enduring scars on your child's body, mind, or emotions.

If you are the parent of a child who is still at home, here are the steps you need to take to achieve healing and prevent further harm:

- Find the courage to say, "I was wrong and I'm sorry!" Be very specific about your mistakes so your child will believe you are honest.
- Offer a brief explanation of why you did the things that were hurtful. It's vital that you do this without defending your actions but in a way that helps your child see she was not a total culprit.
- Work out a plan for changing your old methods. The force of habits makes them hard to break. Unless you show evidence of conscientious work at acquiring new ways, your child may lose trust in your words.
- Seek your child's help in these changes. More effort on his part or a gentle reminder when you slip back into old habits can help you. Such involvement from your child is a great compliment to him.
- In the process of your changing to kinder, gentler ways of training and disciplining, do not become permissive. A child must have rules and boundaries! Just establish them cooperatively and fairly, and enforce them lovingly, firmly, and consistently.

If you are an older person who, like my friends, has lost touch with your angry adult child, here are some ideas for you:

- Never give up reaching out to him, no matter how painful the rejection of you or how untrue and unfair the accusations.
- Think carefully about the growing-up years of your child. Were there times of neglect or undue harshness? You may have focused on the problem behaviors and overlooked your angry punishments or rigid expectations.
- When you are clear about your mistakes, write them out, and include a simple, genuine apology. Offer to discuss the remembered events, and stick with your efforts to make amends. It's easy to deflect such a communication into attempts to make her see *her* mistakes!
- Once you've apologized as earnestly as you can, move on. Don't grovel in past mistakes. Instead write regular brief notes of loving concern for your child's welfare and that of your grandchildren.
- Pray. The power of prayer is immeasurable. What no human being can do is possible with God. I have learned, however, that God will not revoke His gift of the power of choice.

Over time, the healing power of love is difficult to resist. Whether or not your child does so, I can guarantee you will be a better person for choosing to actively love!

Perhaps you are the middle generation person who has discovered memories of past hurts. No matter how tempting it is to stay bitter and unforgiving, please look at the whole picture. The worst mistake often is made out of ignorance or misinformation. Give your child's grandparents a chance to make amends. Confront them clearly and fairly. Share with them your feelings, and ask them specifically for whatever you need to comfort your pain. Set forth some boundaries to protect yourself against further hurts in case they cannot admit their faults or change. Review the steps to forgiveness, and don't confuse the unconditional love this process restores with condoning old mistakes.

No matter how serious your past or current mistakes, no matter how your child may have suffered from those errors, you can change. Healing can take place. The genuineness and the completeness of your changes make the difference. Changing is a major challenge, and your efforts and ultimate success in the process become a superb example for your child.

The age-old story of humankind is this cycle—great potential for good, failure to always measure up, insight and conviction about the need to change, success through redemption, and restoration to the original potential. The grace of forgiving—God's, your child's, and yours—makes this process possible. Often the new relationship that grows out of the healing of the old, broken one through the miracle of forgiveness is filled with richer, more profound love than could be imagined.

Conclusion

Parenting a difficult child is an ongoing challenge draining your energy and exhausting your spirit. Whatever the difficulty —inborn temperament (yours or hers!), personality conflicts, or the unconscious carryover of generations of parenting mistakes—there is hope.

The hope you may count on comes with new information. It grows from the love that overcomes fear and does not need to be defensive. With courage and determination you can bring about the slowly increasing changes that eventually result in joy.

You will need help. And needing help is okay. You don't have to know everything at once, and needing help does not mean you are weak or inadequate. Your child who has seemed to be your greatest problem may, in fact, become your biggest helper. Family members and friends often are waiting for you to ask for their help. You may well find immense benefit from a professional counselor. Above all, remember to consult the wisdom of the heavenly Father.

There are many parents who, like you, struggle with difficult children. Seek them out in your church and school contacts or wherever you meet people. By listening and appropriate sharing, you are likely to discover others who are searching for answers and help. Build a support system where you may discover new ideas, deepen your understanding, and find encouragement.

Seek help through your child's school. A growing number of schools are becoming more aware of the special needs of difficult children. You may find support there, and you also may increase the awareness of the school about such needs. Your parent-teacher-student organization may be able to enrich the resources available for help.

Some churches and a variety of community agencies sponsor seminars on difficult children and their special parenting requirements. Find the time and energy to attend. Parents of really difficult children tell me they are too exhausted by the evening to go to such meetings. I can sympathize with that fatigue. But if, in the long run, it helps you make remedial changes, perhaps the effort will be worthwhile.

Look not only at your problems and your child's. Look also all about you at the resources available and the support of others. You need not face the problems alone. I trust you will find the patient endurance to work through the problems, the strength to care for yourself as well as your difficult child, and in the end, the joy of success at finding the love that truly heals.

Bibliography

Balswick, Jack O., and Judith K. Balswick. *The Family: A Christian Perspective on the Contemporary Home.* Grand Rapids, Mich.: Baker Book House, 1989.

Barnes, Robert G. *You're Not My Daddy: The Step-Parenting Process.* Dallas: Word, 1992.

Chess, Stella, and Alexander Thomas. *Know Your Child: An Authoritative Guide to Today's Parents.* New York: Basic Books, 1987.

Clarke, Jean I. *Self Esteem: A Family Affair.* Minneapolis: Winston Press, 1978.

———, and Connie Dawson. *Growing Up Again.* San Francisco: Harper, 1989.

Cline, Foster, M.D., and Jim Tay. *Parenting with Love and Logic.* Colorado Springs, Colo.: Navpress, 1990.

Driekurs, Rand Soltz. *Children, the Challenge.* Des Moines, Iowa: Meredith, 1964.

Elkind, David. *The Hurried Child: Growing Up Too Fast Too Soon.* Reading, Mass.: Addison-Wesley, 1981.

Encyclopedia of Christian Parenting. Old Tappan, N.J.: Fleming H. Revell, 1982.

Family Matters Handbook, The. Nashville: Thomas Nelson, 1994.

Foward, Susan, and Craig Buck. *Toxic Parents: Overcoming Their Hurtful Legacy and Reclaiming Your Life.* New York: Bantam Books, 1989.

Fulbright, Pat H. *Troubled Teens, Troubled Parents.* Nashville: Broadman Press, 1989.

Gage, Joy P. *When Parents Cry.* Denver: Accent Books, 1980.

Holt, Pat, and Grace Ketterman. *When You Feel Like Screaming.* Wheaton, Ill.: Harold Shaw, 1989.

Jenkins, Jerry, ed. *Families: Practical Advice from More than 50 Experts.* Chicago: Moody Press, 1993.

Ketterman, Grace, M.D. *Choices Are Not Child's Play.* Wheaton, Ill.: Harold Shaw, 1989.

———. *The Complete Book of Baby and Child Care.* Old Tappan, N.J.: Fleming H. Revell, 1984.

———. *Mothering.* Nashville: Thomas Nelson, 1990.

———. *Surviving the Darkness.* Nashville: Thomas Nelson, 1987.

———. *Verbal Abuse.* Ann Arbor, Mich.: Servant/Vine, 1992.

———. *You and Your Child's Problems.* Old Tappan, N.J.: Fleming H. Revell, 1983.

Miller, Stephen M., ed. *Raising Kids.* Kansas City, Mo.: Beacon Hill Press, 1993.

Peck, M. Scott, M.D. *People of the Lie.* New York: Simon and Schuster, 1985.

Scott, Buddy. *Relief for Hurting Parents.* Nashville: Thomas Nelson, 1989.

Turecki, Stanley K., M.D., and Leslie Tanner. *The Difficult Child.* New York: Bantam Books, 1985.

Yorkey, Mike, ed. *Growing a Healthy Home.* Brentwood, Tenn.: Wolgemuth and Hyatt Publishers, 1990.